STORAGE

SCI

2x (3/98) 10/07

Menus For Special Occasions

HISTORIC HOTELS *of* AMERICA

National Trust for Historic Preservation

The Preservation Press

*A*mong the throngs who earn a living doing things culinary, there are a creative few who have the touch to turn a meal into a very special occasion. Collected on these pages are four seasons of such delights for the eye, the palate, and the memory, shared with the reader by the owners, managers, and chefs of 36 historic hotels and restaurants across the country.

Menus For Special Occasions

HISTORIC HOTELS *of* AMERICA

National Trust for Historic Preservation

The Preservation Press

The Preservation Press
National Trust for Historic Preservation
1785 Massachusetts Avenue, N.W.
Washington, D.C. 20036

The National Trust for Historic Preservation is the only private, nonprofit organization chartered by Congress to encourage public participation in the preservation of sites, buildings and objects significant in American history and culture. Support is provided by membership dues, endowment funds, contributions and grants from federal agencies, including the U.S. Department of the Interior, under provisions of the National Historic Preservation Act of 1966. For information about membership, write to the Trust at the above address.

Printed in the United States of America
96 95 94 93 92 5 4 3 2 1

Library of Congress Cataloging-in-Publication Data

Menus for special occasions : historic hotels of America / National Trust for Historic Preservation, the Preservation Press; [compiled and edited by David B. Wolinski].
    p.   cm.
    ISBN 0-89133-173-5 : $29.95
    1. Cookery, American. 2. Menus. 3. Hotels, taverns, etc.—United States.
    I. National Trust for Historic Preservation in the United States.
    II. Wolinski, David B. III. The Preservation Press.
TX715.M558 1992
641.5973—dc20   92-10274

Menus for Special Occasions - Historic Hotels of America
was created for The Preservation Press
by Catling & Company, Baltimore, Md.

CATLING & COMPANY
Executive Editor: Susan J. George
Chairman: Timothy D. Skene Catling
Compiled and Edited by: David B. Wolinski
Art Director: Elizabeth Baile Douglas
Type: William C. Bowie

Printed by the Art Litho Company, Baltimore, Md.

The producers and publishers of this book make no claims to the authenticity, originality, source, or utility of recipes or text submitted by the participants or their representatives.

INTRODUCTION

*H*olidays and special occasions bring families and friends together to enjoy each other and wonderfully prepared food. A beautiful, historic setting can add to the experience. For many, remembering such a festive meal is a sensory pleasure ... a memory that can last a lifetime.

With these thoughts in mind, it gives me great pleasure to introduce the second cookbook from Historic Hotels of America, *Menus for Special Occasions.*

In 1989, the National Trust for Historic Preservation established Historic Hotels of America, an organization that recognizes hotels of exceptional historic architecture and ambience in this country. Hotels from coast to coast, including one in Hawaii, compose this select group. Many of the hotels are hospitality legends. Their very names summon the image of generations of fine American dining experiences.

Menus for Special Occasions gives the flavor of these unique places and how they celebrate. We discover everything from the Fourth of July as it is presented at one hotel in Washington, D.C. (what better place to honor Independence Day?) to a traditional American Thanksgiving at a Midwestern resort. For a somewhat more momentous occasion, consider the menu entitled "The Wedding Day"!

This volume presents a host of pleasing possibilities: 36 varied and tempting menus, each of which tells us something specific about the hotel from which it came, and provides clear, helpful directions for recreating it at home. These are the most obvious rewards of a well-prepared cookbook. Then, there is the intangible reward of being transported to wonderful places with distinct, historical personalities. These are unusual accomplishments for a cookbook, and *Menus for Special Occasions* succeeds at each turn.

Richard B. Barthelmes
Publisher
Gourmet Magazine

TABLE OF CONTENTS

WELCOME
TO HISTORIC HOTELS OF AMERICA

We are pleased to introduce you to Historic Hotels of America™, a program of the National Trust for Historic Preservation. The distinguished hotels featured in this book have accepted our invitation to join an exclusive association—one based on historic character, architectural quality, and the outstanding preservation efforts made by owners and managers who are dedicated to maintaining each hotel's historic integrity.

We have taken care to select hotels that represent a vast cross section of American traveling experiences. Each offers unique accommodations in one-of-a-kind settings, ranging from rustic to refined, in locales as diverse as mountain wilderness, manicured countrysides, the centers of small towns, and bustling metropolises. Though highly diverse, these hotels share a common denominator—a historic environment to enhance your leisure or business trip, coupled with guest services and food and beverage offerings recognized for their outstanding quality.

We invite you to enjoy the hospitality of these fine hotels during your travels. When you do, a portion of your room cost will become a contribution to the National Trust, thus supporting our efforts to preserve America's heritage.

National Trust for Historic Preservation

For information, contact:
Historic Hotels of America
National Trust for Historic Preservation
1785 Massachusetts Avenue, N.W.
Washington, D.C. 20036
202-673-4000

SPRING

A Salem Sea Captain's Dinner

Hawthorne Hotel
Salem, Massachusetts

The Hawthorne Hotel has been a unique and integral part of Salem and Boston's North Shore since being built in the 1920s. Beautifully restored, the stately Federal-style hotel is central to the attractions of historic Salem: the Peabody Museum (the only museum founded by sea captains), the House of the Seven Gables, Pickering Wharf, Salem Harbor, the Salem Maritime Site, and numerous notable sea captains' homes are all within walking distance on the famous Heritage Trail.

The Hawthorne is one of only three Massachusetts hotels selected as a Landmark Lodging Establishment by the state's travelers' guide. Here, they present a Salem sea captain's dinner, reminiscent of the Golden Age of Sail when Salem was one of the largest, most bustling seaports in the country.

Scalloped Oysters
*Shucked Bluepoint Oysters layered with
Cracker Crumbs, Butter, and Cream*

Parsnip Soup

Roast Pheasant
*Whole Pheasant stuffed with Dried Fruit,
roasted and served with Braised Red Cabbage and Apples*

Roast Tenderloin
*Seasoned Tenderloin roasted and sliced,
served with Wild Mushroom Fricassee*

Fresh Brussels Sprouts and Glazed Chestnuts

Apple Charlotte
*Fresh Apples sliced and baked in
Butter-Browned Bread*

COLOR PLATE I

SCALLOPED OYSTERS
Serves 4

½ cup butter
1½ cups cracker crumbs, finely rolled
1½ pints oysters
1½ cups bread crumbs
Salt and freshly ground black pepper
¾ cup oyster liquor
½ cup heavy cream
Buttered bread crumbs
Parsley, chopped

Preheat oven to 400°.
Butter a 1½-quart casserole and cover the bottom with cracker crumbs. Add a layer of ½ the oysters. Make a layer of ½ the bread crumbs, season with salt and pepper, dot with butter, and make an additional layer with the remaining oysters and bread crumbs. Season with salt and pepper, dot with butter. Mix the oyster liquor and cream and pour over the top. Sprinkle with additional buttered bread crumbs and bake 20 to 25 minutes. At service, sprinkle with chopped parsley, serve hot.

PARSNIP SOUP
Serves 5

2 tablespoons butter
½ cup onions, diced
6 parsnips, diced
¼ cup flour
1 quart chicken stock
Salt and pepper
½ cup heavy cream

Melt butter and add onions and parsnips, stir and cook until onions are tender. Add flour, stir and cook for 5 minutes. Add broth, bring to a boil and simmer 15 to 20 minutes. When parsnips are tender, puree the soup in a blender and return to heat, bring to a simmer. Season to taste, add heavy cream in a slow steady stream while stirring. Keep at a low temperature after cream is added.

ROAST PHEASANT
Serves 6

2 whole pheasants, cleaned, giblets removed
2 teaspoons each of salt, pepper, dried sage, and rosemary
Dried Fruit Stuffing

Preheat oven to 325°.
Wash pheasants well under cold water, pat dry. Blend together the seasonings, divide equally and rub the pheasants well with the mixture, including the cavities. Stuff

with Dried Fruit Stuffing, tie.
Place pheasants on a roasting tray and roast, basting often with the juices. Roast approximately 1 hour or until, when pierced, liquids run clear.

DRIED FRUIT STUFFING
For 2 pheasants

1 tablespoon butter
¼ cup dried onions
¼ cup celery, diced
2 cups dried mixed fruits
10 slices white bread, diced
2 eggs, beaten
Chicken stock, as needed
Salt and pepper
1 teaspoon thyme

Melt butter in a saucepan. Add onions, celery, and dried fruit, cook until onions are tender, let cool. Place cooked ingredients in a mixing bowl, add bread and eggs to mixture, mix. Add chicken stock as needed to make the mixture moist. Season to taste with salt and pepper, add thyme. Stuff pheasant and tie.

BRAISED RED CABBAGE
Serves 6

1 head red cabbage, cored, washed
1 large onion, peeled
3 red apples, cored
¼ cup red wine vinegar
1 teaspoon salt
½ teaspoon whole cloves
¼ teaspoon cinnamon
½ teaspoon pepper
1 bottle dry red wine (750 ml)
½ pint fresh raspberries (optional)
4 strips bacon
3 bay leaves

Preheat oven to 375°.
Shred cabbage, onion, and apples. Mix the balance of ingredients (except bacon and bay leaves) with the shredded cabbage. Place in a covered casserole, top with the bacon and bay leaves, braise for approximately 35 to 45 minutes until the mixture is limp and glossy. When ready to serve, remove the bay leaves and what remains of the bacon. Adjust seasonings with salt and pepper, if desired.

Roast Tenderloin
Serves 6

2 tablespoons clarified butter
1 3½-pound centercut tenderloin, fat removed
Salt and pepper

Preheat oven to 400°.

In a heavy skillet, melt the butter and sear beef on all sides. Transfer to a roasting pan, season with salt and pepper, and roast to desired doneness (approximately 15 minutes for rare or until internal temperature reads 120°). Allow to stand for 15 minutes. Reserve drippings from the skillet and roasting pan, discard fat. Slice and serve with Wild Mushroom Fricassee.

❧

Wild Mushroom Fricassee
Serves 6

4 tablespoons butter
1 small onion
1 pound mushroom caps, sliced (any combination of
  domestic or wild mushrooms works well)
½ teaspoon salt
Pepper to taste
Tenderloin drippings (optional)
3 egg yolks
1 tablespoon fresh parsley, chopped
1 tablespoon fresh chives, chopped

Melt butter and sauté onions and mushrooms in a heavy skillet; when liquid begins to form, add salt and pepper. Sauté 1 minute, until mushrooms are soft. Add tenderloin drippings, if desired.

Beat egg yolks and herbs in a small bowl. Temper the yolks by beating a small amount of the mushroom liquid into the eggs, then add the tempered eggs to the mushrooms. Heat slowly, stirring constantly but gently, until slightly thickened (do not allow the fricassee to boil, or it will curdle). Serve with Roast Tenderloin.

Fresh Brussels Sprouts and Glazed Chestnuts
Serves 6

¼ pound chestnuts
2 pounds Brussels sprouts
3 tablespoons butter
¼ cup honey
Salt and pepper
Nutmeg

Peel chestnuts by splitting hull crosswise on flat side with a sharp knife; put chestnuts into boiling salted water, boil for 5 minutes; drain, remove outer shell and skin. Return to the boiling water for 20 minutes, drain.

Peel outer leaves from Brussels sprouts, trim stems. Cut an "x" in the stem of the larger sprouts. Soak in salted water for 10 to 15 minutes. Boil sprouts in water, uncovered, until just tender, 8 to 12 minutes.

Melt butter in a large pan. Add chestnuts and hot Brussels sprouts. Drizzle with the honey, season with salt and pepper and a sprinkling of nutmeg.

❧

Apple Charlotte
Serves 6 to 8

3 tablespoons butter
6 tart apples, cored, peeled, cut into eighths
½ cup sugar
1 tablespoon lemon zest
1 tablespoon orange zest
4 tablespoons apricot preserves
½ cup butter
2 slices white bread, crust removed, each cut
  into 4 triangles
2 slices white bread, crust removed, each cut into halves
Freshly whipped cream

Melt 3 tablespoons butter in a pan and sauté the apples 4 to 5 minutes, stirring constantly. Add sugar and lemon and orange zests, cook 15 minutes, stirring until all the juices have evaporated and the apples are soft. Mix in the apricot preserves.

Preheat oven to 400°.

Butter a 1½-quart charlotte mold. Dip the bread triangles into the melted butter and arrange them in the bottom of the mold allowing the points of the triangles to meet in the center so the bread tightly covers the bottom.

Butter the half slices and arrange them around the edge, overlapping and covering the sides.

Fill the mold with the apple mixture and cover with buttered waxed paper.

Bake for approximately 45 minutes. If the apple mixture shrinks while cooking, fold the bread over the apples.

Allow to cool slightly and invert on a serving platter. Serve warm with freshly whipped cream. ❧

$\mathcal{A}$t $\mathcal{E}$aster

Hotel du Pont
Wilmington, Delaware

Since opening in 1913, the Hotel du Pont has been a Wilmington landmark. Conceived as a hotel of prestige, the public spaces alone required the labors of 18 French and Italian craftsmen for almost two and one-half years to carve, paint, gild, and lay the intricate marble and mosaic floors. A master achievement, the Hotel du Pont was rightfully proclaimed a rival to the finest in Europe.

Two of the Brandywine Valley's finest restaurants are in the hotel. The magnificent Green Room offers outstanding continental cuisine, while classic American specialties are enjoyed in the intimate atmosphere of the Brandywine Room, where original paintings by three generations of Wyeths enhance the decor. The restaurants present this simple yet elegant menu to celebrate spring's most festive holiday.

Wine Soup
Chicken Legs with Savoy Cabbage
Stuffed Easter Capon Roulade
Rhubarb Parfait with Date Soufflé
and Gewürztraminer Sauce

COLOR PLATE 2

Wine Soup
Yield, 1 quart

¼ cup butter
1 tablespoon shallots or onions, chopped
2 tablespoons flour
2 cups chicken stock
1¼ cups dry white wine
1 cup heavy cream
Salt and pepper
Croutons and chopped chives for garnish

Melt butter in pot, add shallots or onions, sauté for approximately 2 minutes. Add flour and mix well. Add chicken stock, wine, and cream together and cook thoroughly, approximately 30 minutes. Season to taste and serve with small toasted croutons and chives.

Chicken Legs with Savoy Cabbage
Serves 4

4 chicken legs
1 leek, sliced
2 carrots, sliced
1 rosemary twig
2 cups chicken stock
¼ pound savoy cabbage
Salt and pepper
4 mushrooms or fresh truffles

Place chicken legs, leeks, carrots, and rosemary twig into hot chicken stock and simmer for about 20 minutes until legs are done, remove vegetables. Blanch cabbage until tender but firm, cut into strips and season with salt and pepper. Place cabbage in large soup plates, place chicken leg on top, garnish with sliced mushrooms or truffles and serve with some of the broth.

Stuffed Easter Capon Roulade
Serves 4

1 large chicken breast, butterflied
Salt and pepper
1 caul fat (order from your local butcher shop), rinsed in water
4 large Swiss chard leaves, ribs removed, blanched
Forcemeat (below)
¼ cup butter
18 dried morels, fresh if available (if dry, soak in water for 3 hours)

Preheat oven to 350°.
Place caul fat on work surface, cover with chard leaf and cover with a thin layer of forcemeat. Place chicken breast on top, fill again and roll. Close up both ends by folding up the caul fat and place into sauté pan. Place in preheated oven, brush with butter and roast for about 20 to 25 minutes. Let rest for about 5 to 8 minutes. Before serving, remove caul fat and slice. Leftover forcemeat can be used to stuff morels and cook for 5 minutes.

Sauce:
Chicken bones and trimmings
6 shallots
1 cup full-bodied red wine
Salt and pepper to taste
4 cups chicken stock
Butter flakes, cold

Chop chicken bones and trimmings, sauté in butter until brown. Add shallots, sauté until shallots brown, deglaze with ⅓ of the red wine. Reduce and deglaze again with the rest of the wine. Reduce, then add chicken stock and simmer for about 30 minutes. Strain through cheesecloth and reduce to about 1 cup.
Before serving, add some cold butter flakes.

Forcemeat:
5 ounces chicken breast
3 ounces chicken livers
Salt and pepper
½ cup heavy cream
2 tablespoons whipped cream
6 to 8 morels, cleaned, washed, blanched
1 slice bread, crust removed, cubed, toasted
1 cup diced carrots, cooked

Cut chicken breast and livers into cubes, season with salt and pepper and heavy cream. Chill well. Use food processor to mix until ingredients are smooth. Fold whipped cream under, add chopped morels, parsley, carrots and croutons.

RHUBARB PARFAIT
Serves 8

½ pound rhubarb, sliced, poached
½ cup beaujolais
¾ cup heavy cream
4 tablespoons sugar
4 egg whites

Poach rhubarb in beaujolais until tender, let cool. Whip heavy cream. Add sugar to egg whites and beat until it forms soft peaks. Fold whipped cream into meringue. Add rhubarb mixture and freeze in a ring mold.

GEWÜRZTRAMINER SAUCE
Yield, 1 cup

⅓ cup simple syrup
1 teaspoon gelatin
1 cup gewürztraminer
¼ lemon, juiced

Gently heat syrup in a saucepan. Dissolve gelatin in a few tablespoons cold water. When softened, blend into syrup to thicken. Allow to cool, add gewürztraminer and lemon juice as noted, or to taste.

DATE SOUFFLÉ
Serves 8

Butter
Hazelnut (filbert) flour
4 egg whites
4 tablespoons sugar
4 egg yolks
2 tablespoons molasses
Zest of ½ lemon
Cinnamon to taste
½ teaspoon vanilla extract
¾ cup bread crumbs
⅓ cup melted butter
1 cup dates, chopped

Preheat oven to 375°.
Smear 8 2½-inch tartlet forms with butter and dust with hazelnut flour. Whip egg whites and sugar into soft peaks. Fold in yolks, molasses, lemon zest, cinnamon, and vanilla. Fold in bread crumbs, melted butter, and dates. Bake in oven in a water bath for about 25 minutes. Serve soufflé hot. ❧

A Day of Country Antiquing

Hotel Northampton
Northampton, Massachusetts

The rich heritage of the Hotel Northampton, built in 1927, owes much to its first manager, Lewis Wiggins. An avid collector of American antiques, Wiggins sought to achieve museum status for the hotel's public rooms and furnishings— by 1937 he employed a full-time antiquarian-curator with a staff of 15. Created from an adjacent century-old structure, the authentic, colonial-styled Wiggins Tavern opened in 1930; in its courtyard the Old Country Store was built, furnished and stocked as a store would have been before 1850.

Located in west-central Massachusetts, the Hotel Northampton is a perfect head-quarters for the day-tripping antique buff, who will find countless interesting shops within easy distance. What better than a delicious picnic smorgasbord to build strength for a busy day of search and discovery?

Soused Salmon

Smoked Salmon Roulade

Three-Pepper Salad
with Strawberry Vinaigrette

Chicken Salad Veronique

Marinated Sliced Beef
in Mustard Vinaigrette

Wiggins Apple Pie

COLOR PLATE 3

Soused Salmon
Serves 4 to 6

1 large salmon steak fillet
1 each: lemon, onion, celery stalk, and carrot, sliced
Pinch dill seed
½ cup vinegar
2 tablespoons water
⅓ cup sugar
10 whole allspice, crushed
5 peppercorns, crushed
2 sprigs fresh dill
2 tablespoons onion, chopped
Fresh dill sprigs and onion rings, for garnish

Clean the salmon steak of bones. Poach in liquid to cover with lemon, onion, celery, carrot, and dill seed. Remove from liquid, cut into thin slices with a sharp knife; slide a spatula under the salmon and remove to a glass dish.

Mix together the remaining ingredients in a saucepan, bring to the boiling point, simmer a few minutes. Cool and strain. Pour the liquid over the salmon and garnish with dill and onion. Chill for 2 hours.

Serve with boiled potatoes or a favorite potato salad.

Smoked Salmon Roulade
filled with Spiced Dungeness Crab
Serves 4

1 cucumber
Salt
1 tablespoon cider vinegar
4 ounces Dungeness crabmeat
2 tablespoons mayonnaise
½ teaspoon salt
1½ tablespoons soy sauce
1 teaspoon fresh ginger, finely diced
¼ teaspoon black pepper
8 to 12 ounces Irish smoked salmon
Sour cream, capers, and parsley sprigs, for garnish

Slice unpeeled cucumber as thin as possible, salt lightly, allow to stand for 20 minutes. Sprinkle with vinegar.

Crumble crabmeat into small pieces. Mix gently with mayonnaise, salt, soy sauce, ginger, and pepper. Divide into 4 equal portions.

Thinly slice smoked salmon into 4 pieces. Top each with ¼ of the crab mixture, roll tightly. Garnish servings with cucumber slices, sour cream, capers, and parsley.

Three-Pepper Salad
Serves 4 to 6

1 each red, green, and yellow bell peppers, seeded, diced
Lettuce, shredded, amount to suit
Red cabbage, shredded, amount to suit
Watercress and diced tomatoes, for garnish

Arrange the diced peppers in straight lines on glass serving plates. Alternate with lines of shredded lettuce and red cabbage. Garnish with watercress and tomatoes. Drizzle Strawberry Vinaigrette over the plates.

(Alternately, you may wish to serve as a tossed salad, by simply tossing the vegetables with the vinaigrette.)

Strawberry Vinaigrette
Yield, 3 cups

1 pint strawberries, hulled, sliced
2 tablespoons sugar
2 cups white wine vinegar
1 cup olive oil

Mix strawberries, sugar, and vinegar in a bowl. Strain through a fine sieve and add 1 cup olive oil. Refrigerate.

Chicken Salad Veronique
Yield, 2 to 4 servings

1 tablespoon curry powder
½ cup mayonnaise
2 chicken breasts, poached, diced
½ cup celery, diced
½ cup seedless white grapes, peeled
Salt and white pepper
Tomato or pineapple, sliced, for garnish

Blend curry powder and mayonnaise in a bowl. Add chicken, celery, and grapes, mix to coat. Season with salt and pepper to taste.

Garnish servings with tomato or pineapple.

MARINATED SLICED BEEF
IN MUSTARD VINAIGRETTE
Serves 4 to 6

2 to 2½ pounds rare roast beef, chilled, thinly sliced

Vinaigrette:

3 ribs celery, julienne

½ cup pecans, chopped

1 scallion, chopped

1 teaspoon shallot, minced

Salt and pepper

2 tablespoons Dijon mustard

1 tablespoon prepared horseradish

1½ tablespoons fresh lemon juice, or vinegar

1 tablespoon fresh parsley, minced

In a large bowl, combine celery, pecans, scallion, shallots, plus salt and pepper to taste. Add balance of ingredients, whisk until well combined.

Pour marinade over the sliced roast beef and marinate 2 to 3 hours, refrigerated. Serve cold.

WIGGINS APPLE PIE
Yield, 1 9-inch pie

12 ounces pastry dough

⅔ to ¾ cup granulated sugar
  (or mix ½ granulated and ½ brown sugar)

1 to 2 tablespoons flour (if fruit is juicy)

⅛ teaspoon salt

1 to 2 tablespoons lemon juice

½ tablespoon lemon zest

¼ tablespoon grated nutmeg

½ tablespoon ground cinnamon

6 to 7 (2 pounds) cooking apples, peeled, thinly sliced

1 tablespoon butter, softened

Preheat oven to 425°.

Equally divide the pastry dough and roll out. Line a 9-inch pie plate with 1 piece.

Combine the filling ingredients except the apples and butter (amount of sugar is determined by the apples' tartness). Place ½ the apples in the lined pie plate. Sprinkle with ½ the sugar mixture. Top with balance of the apples and rest of the sugar mixture, dot with butter.

Top with remaining crust, crimp edges, and egg wash if desired. Bake for 40 to 50 minutes, or until filling is tender and crust is nicely browned. Serve warm.

$\mathcal{A}$ $\mathcal{L}$EISURELY $\mathcal{W}$EEKEND

Lafayette Hotel
Marietta, Ohio

The Lafayette Hotel is located on the banks of the Ohio River in historic Marietta, Ohio. Marietta was the first settlement in the Northwest Territory and is an official stop for the grand riverboats *Mississippi Queen* and *Delta Queen*. The Lafayette, one of the last of the riverboat-era hotels, was named for the 1825 visit of Marquis de Lafayette. In 1992 the owners celebrate the hundredth anniversary of the opening of the hotel, which has long boasted the finest in dining experiences in the Gun Room restaurant. The Gun Room features a collection of steamboat instruments as well as a fine collection of long rifles, including one that accompanied the Benedict Arnold expedition to Quebec in 1775.

Sample these recipes, and dream of a comfortable, relaxing weekend on the historic river.

Oysters with Bacon and Jalapeño

Smoked Rabbit and Oyster Gumbo

Fried Crawfish Salad
with Seasonal Greens and Andouille Dressing

Grilled Fresh Rainbow Trout
with Grilled Spiced Pecans and Tomato Butter Sauce

White Chocolate Brownies
with Dark Chocolate Sauce

Vanilla Bean Ice Cream

COLOR PLATE 4

Oysters with Bacon and Jalapeño
Yield, 24

Rock salt
4 ounces bacon, diced
¼ cup shallots, minced
¼ cup jalapeño peppers, seeded, diced
¼ cup green bell pepper, diced
¼ cup red bell pepper, diced
6 tablespoons butter
6 tablespoons all-purpose flour
2 cups Shrimp Stock (page 118)
1 cup whipping cream
1 6-ounce tomato, peeled, seeded, diced
½ cup Romano cheese, grated
¼ cup hot pepper sauce
Pinch salt
½ cup bread crumbs
¼ teaspoon dried basil, crumbled
1 teaspoon Creole Seasoning (page 110)
1 teaspoon paprika
24 very large oysters
2 tablespoons butter
1 bunch spinach, stemmed
Salt and freshly ground pepper
Fresh thyme sprigs
Lemon halves

Line a baking sheet with ½-inch thick layer of rock salt. Cook bacon in a large heavy skillet over low heat until fat is rendered but bacon is not crisp, stirring frequently, about 15 minutes. Pour off ½ pan drippings. Add shallots, jalapeños, and bell peppers, cook until peppers begin to wilt, about 10 minutes, stirring occasionally.

Create roux by melting butter in a heavy medium saucepan over low heat, add flour and stir 5 minutes, do not brown. Bring stock to boil in another saucepan. Whisk in the roux, add cream and simmer gently 10 minutes, stirring frequently. Strain into skillet with bacon. Stir in tomato and ½ of Romano cheese. Simmer 5 minutes, stirring frequently. Mix in hot pepper sauce and salt.

Combine bread crumbs, ¼ cup Romano cheese, basil, Creole seasoning, and paprika in a small bowl. Open oysters, discard top shells. Remove oysters and drain in a colander, reserve bottom shells. Cook 2 tablespoons butter in a heavy skillet over high heat until beginning to brown. Add spinach and season with salt and pepper. Toss until spinach begins to wilt, about 1 minute. Place bed of spinach on each shell. Top with oyster and arrange on prepared sheet. Sprinkle each with some bread crumb mixture. Top with sauce and additional bread crumbs.

Preheat oven to 450°. Line plates with rock salt. Bake oysters until sauce begins to bubble and tops brown, about 8 minutes. Transfer to prepared plates, garnish with thyme sprigs and lemon, serve.

Smoked Rabbit and Oyster Gumbo
Serves 16

1⅓ cups water
⅔ cup dry white wine
1½ medium onions, thinly sliced
1½ medium heads garlic, halved
2 tablespoons salt
4 teaspoons fresh thyme, chopped
6 bay leaves
6 peppercorns
2 2¼-pound rabbits, each cut into 6 pieces
3 tablespoons Creole Seasoning (page 110)
2 cups hickory or mesquite wood chips,
  soaked in water 30 minutes, drained

Simmer first 8 ingredients for 20 minutes, cool. Place rabbit in a nonreactive pan, pour liquid over rabbit, cover and chill 8 hours, turning occasionally.

Prepare barbeque grill, low heat. Add hickory chips to grill. Drain rabbit, discard marinade. Sprinkle with Creole seasoning. Place rabbit on grill rack, cover and cook approximately 1 hour, or until juices run clear when pricked in the thickest part of the thigh. Cool 1 hour. Remove rabbit meat from bones (reserve for stock). Dice meat into 1-inch cubes.

Gumbo:

2 cups vegetable oil
2⅓ cups all-purpose flour
12 cups Rabbit Stock (page 118)
1½ tablespoons butter
2⅓ cups onion, chopped
2⅓ cups green bell pepper, chopped
⅔ cup celery, chopped
4 teaspoons fresh thyme, chopped
3 bay leaves
1½ pounds beefsteak tomatoes, peeled, seeded,
  diced, well drained
24 oysters, shucked, liquor reserved
1⅓ cups green onion, chopped
2 tablespoons Tabasco
2 tablespoons filé powder
Salt
Cooked white rice

Heat oil in a heavy saucepan over medium-high heat until almost smoking. Using a wooden spoon, carefully incorporate flour. Reduce heat to low and stir constantly until roux is dark brown, about 10 minutes. Whisk roux into rabbit stock and simmer 15 minutes, strain through a sieve and keep warm.

Meanwhile, melt butter in another large saucepan over medium-low heat. Add onion, bell pepper, celery, thyme, and bay leaves. Cook until vegetables are tender. Add stock and tomatoes and simmer 35 minutes. Add rabbit meat and oysters, oyster liquor, green onions, Tabasco, filé powder, and salt. Increase heat to boil, reduce heat and simmer 5 minutes. Adjust seasonings.

(Continued, page 14.)

To serve, place a small mound of cooked rice in each bowl. Ladle gumbo over and around, garnish with additional chopped green onion, if desired.

❧

FRIED CRAWFISH SALAD
WITH SEASONAL GREENS
Serves 4

1 pound crawfish, shelled
⅓ cup Louisiana hot sauce
8 cups mixed bitter greens (red leaf lettuce, romaine, radicchio, arugula, escarole, etc.)
2 beefsteak tomatoes, sliced
2 cups all-purpose flour
½ cup cornstarch
1 tablespoon Creole Seasoning (page 110)
Vegetable oil, for deep frying

Marinate crawfish in hot sauce while preparing salad greens. Wash greens and dry between paper towels. Divide tomatoes among plates, using them as a decorative border. Divide greens among plates.

Heat oil to 350° in a deep fryer or saucepan.

Drain crawfish. Mix flour, cornstarch, and Creole seasoning in a medium bowl. Dredge crawfish in flour mixture, shake off excess. Fry in batches (do not crowd) until golden brown, about 2 minutes. Drain on paper towels.

Spoon desired amount of Andouille Dressing over greens. Top with crawfish, serve.

ANDOUILLE DRESSING
Yield, about 3 cups

1 slice bacon, finely diced
6 ounces Andouille sausage, diced (Smoked Hungarian sausage or kielbasa may be substituted)
⅓ cup onion, diced
1 teaspoon brown sugar
1 clove garlic, minced
⅓ cup white vinegar
1 tablespoon Louisiana hot sauce
2 egg yolks, room temperature
1 tablespoon Creole mustard
2¼ cups vegetable oil
⅓ cup red wine vinegar
Salt and freshly ground pepper

Cook bacon in a heavy skillet over medium heat until lightly browned. Add sausage and heat through, about 2 minutes. Add onion and stir 1 minute. Stir in sugar, garlic, white vinegar, and hot sauce. Simmer 1 minute, remove from heat, cool slightly.

Combine yolks and mustard in a bowl. Gradually whisk in ½ of the oil in a thin stream. Whisk in red wine vinegar, then remaining oil. Stir in bacon/sausage

mixture, salt and pepper to taste.

The dressing may be made a few days early and refrigerated.

❧

GRILLED FRESH RAINBOW TROUT
Serves 6

6 ¾- to 1-pound fresh trout, boned, butterflied
Melted butter
Creole Seasoning (page 110)
Hickory chips for barbecuing, water soaked, drained
Tomato Butter Sauce (page 110)
Grilled Spiced Pecans
Tomato slices, grilled (optional)
Pattypan squash, steamed (optional)
Basil sprigs, for garnish

Prepare a hot barbeque grill.

Brush trout with butter, sprinkle with seasoning. Add hickory chips to grill. Set trout on grill skin-side up. Cover and cook until just opaque, 2½ minutes per side.

Ladle Tomato Butter Sauce on plates. Place trout on sauce, top with Spiced Pecans. If desired, garnish with grilled tomatoes, steamed squash and basil sprigs.

GRILLED SPICED PECANS
Serves 6

1 cup pecan halves, coarsely chopped
2 tablespoons butter, melted
1 teaspoon fresh thyme, minced
1 teaspoon fresh oregano, minced
½ teaspoon Creole Seasoning (page 110)
¼ teaspoon allspice
Hickory or mesquite chips, water soaked for 30 minutes, drained

Prepare a low-heat barbeque grill. Pierce holes in a disposable aluminium baking pan. Mix first 6 ingredients, spread out on the baking pan. Add 1 cup wood chips to the grill, place pan on grill. Cover and smoke until pecans are toasted, about 30 minutes, stirring occasionally. Add chips as necessary to maintain smoke. Remove pecans from grill, keep warm. ❧

TOMATO BUTTER SAUCE
page 110

WHITE CHOCOLATE BROWNIES
page 110

DARK CHOCOLATE SAUCE
page 110

VANILLA BEAN ICE CREAM
page 111

A Hiker's Holiday

Mohonk Mountain House
New Paltz, New York

At Mohonk, 85 miles of circuitous trails meander amidst thousands of mountaintop acres of unsurpassed natural beauty. Rocky cliffs rise dramatically above a crystal blue lake surrounded by lush forest. In 1869, this scene inspired Albert and Alfred Smiley to create Mohonk Mountain House, where people and nature flourish in harmony.

The Mountain House is a turreted 275-room architectural delight reaching seven stories skyward and stretching an eighth of a mile along Lake Mohonk. Hikers of all ages and abilities can make their way to a favorite gazebo view with a specially prepared picnic lunch to enjoy a feast for body and soul. The natural beauties found at Mohonk have been honored by its designation as a National Historic Landmark.

Smoked Trout Salad with Fresh Melon
Hearty Pheasant Lentil Stew
Whole Grain Biscuits
Roquefort Chutney Spread
Chocolate Nut Torte
Minted Iced Tea

COLOR PLATE 5

Smoked Trout Salad with Fresh Melon
Serves 4

3 tablespoons fresh apple juice
1 tablespoon raspberry vinegar
¼ cup olive oil
Salt and pepper
1 teaspoon dill weed, chopped
¼ cantaloupe, rind removed, seeded
¼ honeydew, rind removed, seeded
½ medium white onion, diced
4 fillets of smoked trout, crumbled

Create a vinaigrette by whisking together the apple juice and vinegar in a bowl. Continue whisking while slowly adding olive oil. Salt and pepper to taste. Add dill.

Dice melons into ½-inch cubes. Combine melons, onion and trout in a serving dish, drizzle with the vinaigrette.

Hearty Pheasant Lentil Stew
Serves 4

4 tablespoons butter
3 small leeks, well rinsed, chopped
3 carrots, peeled, diced
2 onions, diced
4 cloves garlic, minced
6 cups chicken stock
1 pheasant, cleaned, split
½ cup dry red lentils
½ cup dry green lentils
4 tablespoons Italian parsley, chopped
Salt and pepper

Melt butter in a large saucepan over medium high heat. Add leeks, carrots, onions, and garlic, sauté until vegetables wilt, about 10 minutes. Add chicken stock, lentils, and pheasant. Simmer for ½ hour, stirring occasionally.

Remove pheasant from stock, remove meat from bones. Return meat to the stock and garnish with parsley. Serve hot. Salt and pepper to taste.

Whole Grain Biscuits
Yield, 1 dozen

1 cup bread flour
1 cup bulghur or whole wheat flour
1 cup rye flour
2 tablespoons baking powder
⅓ teaspoon salt
½ cup shortening
1¼ cups milk

Preheat oven to 350°.

Combine dry ingredients, mix in shortening and milk. Mix until it is moist.

Roll out dough to a ¾-inch thickness. Cut into 3- to 4-inch circles. Bake on parchment paper for 12 to 16 minutes.

Serve warm, split.

Roquefort Chutney Spread
Yield, 2 cups

½ pound Roquefort cheese
2 tablespoons cream cheese
¼ cup white raisins
1 mango, peeled, seeded
½ teaspoon ginger, grated
2 tablespoons sherry vinegar
¼ teaspoon turmeric
Salt and pepper

Combine all ingredients in a food processor using a plastic blade. Mix until well combined but not smooth.

Serve as a spread for crackers, biscuits or bread.

Chocolate Nut Torte
Yield, 1 10-inch torte

2½ sticks unsalted butter
1⅓ cups granulated sugar
1⅓ cups almond paste
10 eggs
1 cup cake crumbs
2 teaspoons baking powder
2 cups pecan pieces
¾ cup cocoa powder
Confectioners' sugar, for topping

Preheat oven to 325°.

Have butter at room temperature, cream together with sugar and almond paste. Add eggs, sift in the cake crumbs, cocoa, and baking powder. Mix in pecan pieces.

Bake in a greased and floured 10-inch cake pan for 1 hour. Dust with confectioners' sugar.

A Prenuptial Dinner

Omni Netherland Plaza
Cincinnati, Ohio

O rchids is a highly acclaimed restaurant devoted to producing the finest cooking of Midwestern America. Recently, the noted expert on the cooking of this area, Richard Perry, became the restaurateur for Orchids. A member of the Fine Dining Hall of Fame and the First Fifty Who's Who of Cooking in America, he brings his broad experience to one of America's premier restaurants. His cooking reflects Midwest life, and many recipes are derived from those found in the finest turn-of-the-century homes, hotels, and riverboats in the region. Dishes are home-spun and familiar, yet complex and sophisticated.

The area's finest produce — prepared by a highly trained staff and served with elegance and flair by the finest team in Cincinnati — Orchids at the Omni Netherland Plaza.

Shrimp and Avocado Salad

Breast of Capon Stuffed with Morels
with Honey-Mustard Sauce

Broccoli
with Black Walnut Butter

Potatoes Byron

Ozark Corn Chowder

Cracked Wheat Bread
with Pear Butter

Bourbon Chiffon Pie

Summer Pudding

COLOR PLATE 6

SHRIMP AND AVOCADO SALAD

For each serving:
½ large avocado
½ cup Marinated Shrimp
¼ cup Dill Mayonnaise
Lettuce of your choice

Peel the avocado; cut it into pieces and fold with the remaining ingredients; serve on a bed of crisp chilled lettuce.

MARINATED SHRIMP
Serves 12

9 tablespoons olive oil
6 tablespoons white wine vinegar
3 teaspoons Dijon mustard
3 pounds shrimp, peeled, deveined, cooked

Combine oil, vinegar, and mustard; whisk well until blended; cool the cooked shrimp and cut it into chunks; add them to the liquid; stir to coat; put in a container, cover and refrigerate for at least 2 hours.

DILL MAYONNAISE
Yield, about 3½ cups

3 cups mayonnaise
6 tablespoons chili sauce
3 large cloves garlic, crushed
1 tablespoon Tabasco
½ tablespoon salt
¼ tablespoon black pepper
6 tablespoons dried dill leaves
6 tablespoons fresh chives, chopped
2 tablespoons fresh lemon juice

Combine all ingredients, cover and refrigerate.

BROCCOLI WITH BLACK WALNUT BUTTER

For each serving:
¼ cup fresh broccoli florets, cooked
1 tablespoon Black Walnut Butter

Steam the broccoli so that it remains bright green and is still crisp; stir in the hot Black Walnut Butter and serve topped with walnuts.

BLACK WALNUT BUTTER
Yield, 1½ cups

8 cups black walnuts
1½ cups clarified butter

Simmer the walnuts and butter on very low heat for 1½ hours. Strain, keep flavored butter and nuts separate.

BONELESS BREAST OF CAPON STUFFED WITH MORELS
Serves 12

¾ cup onions, chopped
2½ cups fresh morels, chopped
2 tablespoons clarified butter
1 tablespoon fresh lemon juice
6 12-ounce breasts of capon, boned, skinned, split
Seasonal herbs and vegetables, for garnish

Sauté onions and morels in clarified butter, add lemon juice, put the mixture in a clean cheesecloth and squeeze to remove all the moisture.

Preheat oven to 375°.

Pound the half breasts between sheets of plastic wrap until they are ⅛-inch thick. Place 2 of the half breasts together, overlapping by ¾ inch to prevent them from coming apart when rolled. Spread the mushroom mixture on the bottom half of the capon breasts, roll up jelly-roll style. Bake for 15 to 20 minutes until done, but still juicy.

To serve, place the Honey Mustard Sauce on a heated plate. Slice the capon and place several slices on top of the sauce; garnish with seasonal herbs and vegetables and serve.

HONEY-MUSTARD SAUCE
Yield, about 3 cups

2 tablespoons shallots, minced
2 tablespoons clover honey
½ cup Ozark mustard
1 tablespoon honey vinegar, or other white vinegar
1 cup chicken stock
1 cup dry white wine
1 teaspoon paprika
½ teaspoon salt
¼ teaspoon pepper
2 cups heavy cream

Combine all ingredients, except heavy cream; reduce in a saucepan over high heat until ½ the mixture remains; add the heavy cream and boil until the mixture is thick and rich.

POTATOES BYRON
Serves 8

5 pounds baking potatoes
Salted water
1 pound butter
2 cups Gruyère cheese, grated
3 tablespoons salt
1 tablespoon black pepper, cracked
2 cups heavy cream

Peel the potatoes and cut into 1-inch chunks; blanch the potatoes in salted water. As soon as the potatoes are tender, drain them thoroughly, place them in the bottom of a greased baking pan.

Cut the butter into chunks and mix it into the potatoes; lightly stir in the grated Gruyère cheese; season with salt and pepper; pour the cream over the mixture and let sit at room temperature for ½ hour.

Preheat oven to 375°.

Bake uncovered until the potatoes heat through, the cheese melts, and a golden crust forms.

OZARK CORN CHOWDER
Serves 10

10 strips bacon
¾ cup onion, minced
1¼ cups celery, chopped
2½ cups parsley root, sliced
5 cups fresh whole kernel white sweet corn
5 cups water
5 cups heavy cream
5 tablespoons butter
5 tablespoons flour
1 tablespoon salt
1 teaspoon black pepper

Crisp the bacon in a skillet; crumble and reserve bacon; pour off all but ¼ cup of the bacon fat; sauté the onions and celery in the bacon fat. Combine the sautéed onions and celery with the corn, parsley root, and water, bring to a boil and simmer until the parsley root is tender. Make a roux of the butter and flour; add to the soup and simmer until thickened. Add the remaining ingredients, including the crumbled bacon; reheat, but be careful not to boil.

BOURBON CHIFFON PIE
Yield, 2 9- to 10-inch pies

Crust:
2½ cups graham cracker crumbs
½ cup sugar
1 teaspoon nutmeg
½ cup melted butter

Preheat oven to 350°.

Combine graham cracker crumbs, sugar, and nutmeg; moisten with melted butter and mold in pie pan; bake until lightly golden.

Filling:
2 envelopes unflavored gelatin
1 cup black coffee
⅔ cup sugar
¼ teaspoon salt
6 egg yolks, beaten
10 tablespoons bourbon
½ cup Kahlúa
3 egg whites
⅔ cup sugar
2½ cups heavy cream

Combine gelatin, coffee, ⅔ cup sugar, and salt; bring to a simmer. Temper egg yolks with the hot liquid, blend both liquids. Carefully heat resulting mixture and whisk; allow to cool and add bourbon and Kahlúa.

Make a meringue with the egg whites and sugar; whip the heavy cream; fold into the other mixture; put in pie shells and chill 24 hours.

SUMMER PUDDING
Serves 8

3 cups fresh berries (blackberries, raspberries, etc.)
⅔ cup sugar
6 thick slices homemade white bread

Cook the berries and sugar for 5 to 10 minutes on low heat; strain, reserve both the berries and the juice. Trim the crusts from the bread; line the bottom and sides of a deep cake mold with the bread, making sure that the pieces overlap and that it is pressed into shape, but not smashed; add the berries and some of the juice; put bread on the top of the filled mold; add remaining juice; weight down the entire pudding with a heavy weight and refrigerate overnight.

Unmold the pudding on a plate; slice and serve. ❧

CRACKED WHEAT BREAD
page 114

PEAR BUTTER
page 114

A Springtime Affair

Pinehurst Resort & Country Club
Pinehurst, North Carolina

Since the hotel's grand opening on New Year's Day, 1901, the coming of spring in Pinehurst brings many wonderful events to this historic area. Springtime means the azaleas are in bloom, the grass gets greener, and golfers return to Pinehurst's legendary courses. Springtime also brings the return of many great social events such as Stonybrook Steeplechase and Polo for the Arts. This is the time of year for you to open up your home and heart to old friends and to celebrate with extraordinary cuisine. As you look over the menu you will notice that the ingredients are basic to the great Southern culinary tradition — peaches, pungent herbs, fresh seafood, pecans — equally timeless staples of the Pinehurst kitchens.

Pinehurst Peach Compote
*with Cinnamon Yogurt Cream
and Brandied Sun-Dried Cherries*

Cape Hatteras Black Grouper Steamed in Clay
with Blackeyed Peas-and-Thyme Relish

Pecan Nougat Torte

COLOR PLATE 7

PINEHURST PEACH COMPOTE WITH CINNAMON YOGURT CREAM AND BRANDIED SUN-DRIED CHERRIES
Serves 12

Peach puree:
12 fresh peaches
2 cinnamon sticks
½ teaspoon cinnamon
½ teaspoon nutmeg
3 lemons, juiced
1 cup peach schnapps

Clean, peel, and remove pits from peaches; stew with rest of ingredients for 10 minutes. Puree in a food processor, cool.

Cinnamon Yogurt Cream:
¼ teaspoon cinnamon
¼ cup Grand Marnier
2 cups plain yogurt
Mint, for garnish

Dissolve cinnamon in Grand Marnier and whip in yogurt.

Brandied Cherries:
¼ cup sun-dried cherries
2 tablespoons brandy

Marinate sun-dried cherries in brandy overnight.

To serve:

Fill 12 fluted champagne glasses with alternating layers of peach puree and yogurt cream, topping with yogurt cream. Decorate each serving with the marinated cherries and a sprig of mint.

CAPE HATTERAS BLACK GROUPER STEAMED IN CLAY
Serves 2

2 7-ounce portions fresh grouper, scaled
Fresh dill
Sea salt
Baking paper
2 tablespoons butter
Fresh thyme
2 pieces of potter's clay, rolled ⅜-inch thick and
  9 inches in diameter

Rub skin of grouper generously with dill and sea salt. Place in baking paper with butter and thyme, wrap.

Place grouper on 1 piece of the clay. Top with the other piece of clay, pressing to remove air and creating a clay envelope. If you wish, use the point of a knife to incise a decorative pattern on the clay. (The clay-wrapped fish should be refrigerated if not immediately used.)

At serving time, preheat oven to 550º.

Place the fish on a baking sheet and bake for 15 minutes. When it is taken from the oven, break the clay to remove the grouper. Remove baking paper and skin. Place on plates, serve with Blackeyed Peas-and-Thyme Relish, garnish with a sprig of thyme.

BLACKEYED PEAS-AND-THYME RELISH
Yield, approximately 3 cups

¾ cup blackeyed peas
2½ cups chicken stock
½ red bell pepper, medium diced
½ green bell pepper, medium diced
½ yellow bell pepper, medium diced
1 shallot, diced
1 teaspoon garlic, diced
2 teaspoons fresh thyme
1 tablespoon pickle relish, pureed
1 tablespoon cider vinegar

Soak peas in water overnight, drain. Cook peas in stock until softened, allow to cool. Mix in balance of ingredients, marinate overnight.

Linzer Dough

Yield, 2 10-inch crusts

1 cup butter
¾ cup sugar
1 egg
1 cup hazelnuts, finely chopped
1 teaspoon cinnamon
1 teaspoon baking powder
1 teaspoon vanilla extract
2 cups cake flour

Use a paddle in a mixing bowl to cream together the butter, sugar, and egg, until fluffy. Add the chopped hazelnuts, mix for about 30 seconds. Blend in the cinnamon, baking powder, and vanilla. Add the cake flour and mix 1 to 2 minutes, until a ball is formed. Cover or wrap in plastic, refrigerate for at least ½ hour.

Pecan Nougat Torte

Yield, 1 10-inch torte

2¼ cups sugar
½ cup water
1½ cups heavy cream
1 pound pecan pieces
Zest of 1 lemon
Egg wash (1 egg mixed with 1 tablespoon water)
1 recipe Linzer Dough

Cook sugar and water in a saucepot until sugar turns to a caramel stage (golden brown), 325° to 350° on a candy thermometer.

Add the cream a little at a time and stir until mixed, taking caution not to be splashed by the hot sugar. When all the cream has been incorporated, remove from heat and add the pecan pieces and lemon zest. Stir until mixed, set aside to cool.

Divide chilled dough in half. Roll out each portion to about ⅛-inch thick and slightly more than 10 inches across. Roll dough around rolling pin and place dough over a 10-inch tart shell with removable bottom, allowing excess dough to hang over edges of the pan.

Fill the shell with the nougat mixture. Egg wash the edge of the shell and cover with the second piece of dough. Press edges to seal, then use rolling pin to trim excess dough.

Preheat oven to 350°.

Egg wash the top of the shell completely. Place on a sheet pan and bake for 35 to 40 minutes or until dough is golden. Remove from oven, set aside to cool. ❧

Photography: Barry Berenson, at the House of the Seven Gables

COLOR PLATE 1   A SALEM SEA CAPTAIN'S DINNER   PAGE 3
Hawthorne Hotel

L/R: Roast Tenderloin, Apple Charlotte, Brussels Sprouts with Chestnuts,
Roast Pheasant with Dried Fruit Stuffing and Braised Cabbage and Apples, Scalloped Oysters

Photography: Du Pont External Affairs

Hotel du Pont

L/R: Chicken Legs with Savoy Cabbage, Datenut Souffle and Rhubarb Parfait
with Gewürztraminer Sauce, Stuffed Capon Roulade, Wine Soup

COLOR PLATE 3   A DAY OF COUNTRY ANTIQUING
Hotel Northampton

L/R: Wiggins Apple Pie, Salmon Roulade, Chicken Salad Veronique,
Three-Pepper Salad, Soused Salmon, Marinated Beef

A LEISURELY WEEKEND
Lafayette Hotel

L/R: Grilled Trout with Pecans and Tomato Butter Sauce, Oysters with Bacon and Jalapeño

COLOR PLATE 5

A HIKER'S HOLIDAY
Mohonk Mountain House

L: Chocolate Nut Torte

Omni Netherland Plaza

L/R: Breast of Capon Stuffed with Morels, Broccoli with Black Walnut Butter, Ozark Corn Chowder

A SPRINGTIME AFFAIR
Pinehurst Resort & Country Club

L/R: Cape Hatteras Black Grouper Steamed in Clay, Blackeyed Peas-and-Thyme Relish,
Pinehurst Peach Compote, Pecan Nougat Torte

The Sagamore, an Omni Classic Resort

L/R: Mushroom Potatoes and Tomatoes Provençal with Fresh Asparagus, Sirloin with Kale, Speckled Vanilla Ice Cream, Strawberry and Rhubarb Crisp, Popovers, Hoppin' John Salad, Shrimp and Hushpuppies

A Cruise on the Lake

The Sagamore — an Omni Classic Resort
Bolton Landing, New York

The Sagamore is a year-round luxury resort located on a 70-acre island in Lake George, in the heart of the Adirondack Mountains. Originally built in 1883, the resort underwent a $75-million restoration, completed in 1985. Listed in the National Register of Historic Places, the 350-room resort is equipped with a state-of-the-art conference center and a full range of recreational facilities including an 18-hole championship golf course by Donald Ross, tennis, racquetball, an indoor/outdoor heated pool, and The Sagamore Spa — a full-service health and fitness club — plus numerous lakefront activities.

A favorite attraction for guests during the spring and summer months is *The Morgan*, a 72-foot yacht offering a unique setting for lunch or dinner while cruising the placid waters of Lake George.

Barbequed Smoked Shrimp with Hushpuppies

Hoppin' John Salad
with Melon and Smithfield Ham

Peppered Sirloin Steak
with Pan-Fried Kale and Whiskey Sauce

Roasted Mushroom Potatoes
Fried Tomatoes Provençal
Fresh Asparagus

Deep Dish Strawberry and Rhubarb Crisp
with Speckled Vanilla Ice Cream

Warm Buttered Popovers

COLOR PLATE 8

BARBEQUED SMOKED SHRIMP
Serves 6

18 U-15 (jumbo) green headless shrimp, peeled,
  butterflied, tails on
1½ cups barbeque sauce
2 tablespoons liquid smoke
½ cup clarified butter
¾ cup mango chutney
12 hushpuppies
Fresh thyme or rosemary garnish

*Marinate shrimp in ⅓ of the barbeque sauce and the
liquid smoke for at least 4 hours.*

*Add clarified butter to a very hot skillet. Sauté the
marinated shrimp quickly, letting them caramelize to a
golden red-brown and fully cook. Remove from heat, keep
warm.*

*Heat remaining barbeque sauce. Assemble shrimp on
a serving platter with the mango chutney. Drizzle shrimp
with heated sauce. Serve with Hushpuppies, garnish with
fresh herbs.*

HUSHPUPPIES
Yield, 12 hushpuppies

2 cups yellow cornmeal
1 teaspoon baking powder
1 cup milk
½ teaspoon salt
2 eggs, beaten
½ cup onion, finely chopped
Shortening or cooking oil

*Mix ingredients well, to an extra heavy consistency.
Allow mixture to rest 5 minutes.*

*Shape into rounded teaspoon ovals, pan fry in hot oil
until golden brown. Drain hushpuppies on paper towels
or parchment paper. Serve warm.*

HOPPIN' JOHN SALAD
WITH MELON AND SMITHFIELD HAM
Serves 6

1¾ cups cooked white rice
1¼ cups cooked blackeyed peas
1 cup honey vinaigrette dressing (⅓ cup each honey,
  vinegar, and salad oil)
¼ cup green pepper, diced
¼ cup red pepper, diced
1 tablespoon parsley, chopped
Salt and pepper to taste

*Combine the ingredients in a bowl and season to
taste, chill completely.*
6 radicchio leaves
6 bibb lettuce leaves
6 medium slices honeydew melon
6 medium slices cantaloupe
6 ½-ounce portions Smithfield ham, shaved
Fresh mint for garnish

*Arrange serving plates with radicchio and lettuce
leaves, top with Hoppin' John Salad. Place melon slices
next to the salad, top salad with ham shavings, garnish
with mint. Serve cold.*

PEPPERED SIRLOIN STEAK
WITH PAN-FRIED KALE AND WHISKEY SAUCE
Serves 6

¾ cup black peppercorns, crushed
6 8-ounce New York sirloin steaks
Salt to taste
Clarified butter

Whiskey Sauce:
¼ cup whiskey
1½ cups demi-glace
6 ounces fresh kale

*Equally distribute peppercorns on both sides of steaks,
pressing to adhere. Salt lightly if desired. Sauté steaks in
clarified butter in a hot pan, browning both sides to
desired doneness. Remove from pan, keep warm.*

*Deglaze pan with whiskey, flaming to remove alcohol.
Add demi-glace, let reduce 2 to 3 minutes, season to taste,
keep hot.*

*Quickly pan fry the kale in a hot skillet with clarified
butter until tender, season to taste. Top steaks with the
kale and drizzle with the sauce, serve immediately.*

ROASTED MUSHROOM POTATOES
Serves 6

12 medium red bliss potatoes
¼ cup olive oil
Salt and pepper
Vegetable oil

Preheat oven to 375°.
*Use a paring knife to peel a strip around the potatoes,
shaping to resemble mushrooms with stems, leaving the
red jacket skin on top of the "mushroom." Rinse in cold
water and drain well. Put potatoes in a bowl and add
olive oil, salt and pepper lightly, and toss until coated.*

*Roast potatoes on a sheet lightly oiled with vegetable
oil until tender and golden brown. Serve hot.*

Fried Tomatoes Provençal
Serves 6

Breaded tomatoes:
2 medium whole tomatoes
Salt, pepper, and oregano
Flour
2 eggs
¼ cup milk
Seasoned bread crumbs
1 cup olive oil

Cut the ends from each tomato, cut each tomato into 3 thick slices; season to taste with salt, pepper, and oregano. Dredge slices in flour and remove excess. Beat eggs with milk, dip tomatoes in the mixture and shake off excess. Place tomatoes in bread crumbs, shake off excess.

Sauté tomatoes in olive oil until golden brown; drain on parchment paper. Serve hot, topped with concasse.

Seasoned concasse:
¼ cup olive oil
2 teaspoons garlic, chopped
1½ cups tomato concasse (tomatoes peeled, seeded, finely chopped)
¼ cup tomato paste
1 tablespoon parsley, chopped
Salt and pepper

Heat olive oil over medium-high heat and sauté garlic, taking care not to brown or burn. Add tomato concasse and simmer 5 minutes. Add tomato paste and parsley, salt and pepper to taste. Cook an additional 3 minutes.

❧

Fresh Asparagus
Serves 6

18 medium asparagus spears
¼ cup butter
Salt and pepper

Lightly peel the ends of the asparagus, trimming bottoms for uniformity.

Bring a pot of lightly salted water to boil, add asparagus. Cook for 3 to 4 minutes until tender yet firm, drain.

Melt butter in a wide pan. Add asparagus, salt and pepper to taste, toss gently. Serve immediately.

❧

Warm Buttered Popovers
page 110

Deep Dish Strawberry and Rhubarb Crisp
Yield, 1 9-inch deep-dish pie

Filling:
1 cup sugar
1 cup water
2 cups rhubarb, angle sliced
¼ cup grenadine syrup
Zest of ½ lemon
Zest of ½ orange
3 tablespoons arrowroot or cornstarch
50 medium strawberries, hulled, halved

Topping:
½ cup gingersnap crumbs, ground
¾ cup graham cracker crumbs, ground
¼ cup light brown sugar
1 cup unsalted butter, melted
Confectioners' sugar

Dissolve and heat sugar in water to a syrup consistency. Add rhubarb and cook over medium heat until tender, but still firm. Add grenadine, and lemon and orange zests.

Make a thin paste of the arrowroot and a little cold water. Add the arrowroot to the mixture and continue to heat and stir until well thickened. Gently fold in strawberries and heat for about 1½ minutes; remove from heat, set aside.

For the topping, blend together the crumbs and brown sugar. Add melted butter, blend to a wet sand consistency.

Preheat oven to 350°.

Place the filling in a 9- to 10-inch deep-dish ceramic pie plate or casserole, cover with the prepared topping. Bake for about 20 minutes, until the topping is golden brown; dust with confectioners' sugar. Serve warm with Speckled Vanilla Ice Cream.

❧

Speckled Vanilla Ice Cream
Yield, 1 gallon

1 quart milk
1 quart heavy cream
2 cups sugar
16 egg yolks
½ cup speckled vanilla extract

In a heavy-bottomed saucepot, bring milk, cream, and ½ of the sugar to a boil. Blend egg yolks with remaining sugar and temper with a small amount of the boiling cream mixture. Add the tempered egg and sugar mixture to the hot milk. Cook over low heat, stirring constantly with a spoon, until thickened. Flavor with the vanilla extract, incorporate and mix well.

Remove the mixture from the heat and strain. Cool the ice cream over an ice bath, and process in an ice cream freezer according to manufacturer's instructions. ❧

$\mathcal{A}$ Brunch with Friends

The Saint Paul Hotel
St. Paul, Minnesota

Overlooking Rice Park and the renowned Ordway Music Theatre, The Saint Paul offers unmatched vistas of the Twin Cities. Financed by the St. Paul Business League, and designed by Reed and Stern of Grand Central Station fame, this landmark hotel opened in 1910.

James J. Hill, noted philanthropist, was host to the gala grand opening — 6,000 American Beauty roses adorned the interior. Friends of F. Scott Fitzgerald gathered at the hotel in 1920 at his return from Princeton. The hotel was host to Little Falls native, Charles Lindbergh, on his triumphant return. Sinclair Lewis resided at The Saint Paul in 1921 while filming *Free Air*.

For 80 years, social history has been made at The Saint Paul. What better spot to enjoy a leisurely brunch with business associates and close friends?

Fresh Seasonal Fruit
with Devonshire Cream

Grilled Tuna Salad
on Mixed Greens with Dijon Vinaigrette

Tenderloin Eggs Benedict
with Hashed Brown Potatoes and Cream
and Apple-Cinnamon Coffee Cake

Chocolate Pecan Pie
with Kentucky Bourbon Sauce

COLOR PLATE 9

FRESH SEASONAL FRUIT
WITH DEVONSHIRE CREAM
Yield, approximately 3 cups

Devonshire Cream:
½ cup heavy cream
1 cup sour cream
¼ cup brown sugar
⅓ cup Amaretto

Whip cream until double in volume and firm. Add sour cream, brown sugar, and Amaretto. Mix on low speed until fully incorporated, chill. Serve over your choice of fresh sliced fruits.

❧

GRILLED TUNA SALAD
Serves 6

1 head bibb lettuce, leaves separated
9 cups mixed greens of choice, washed, dried
12 eggs, boiled, quartered
12 cucumber slices
12 tomato wedges
6 4-ounce Ahi tuna steaks, sushi quality
½ cup olive oil
1½ cups Dijon Vinaigrette

Put 2 leaves bibb lettuce on individual plates, top with 1½ cups mixed greens. Divide and arrange egg quarters, cucumbers, and tomatoes on perimeters of plates, refrigerate.

Coat tuna steaks in olive oil and sauté or grill to medium rare. Slice into ¼-inch strips. Top salads with the tuna, dress each with ¼ cup Dijon Vinaigrette, serve.

DIJON VINAIGRETTE
Yield, 2 cups

4 egg yolks
1 bulb shallot, peeled
1 teaspoon garlic, peeled, chopped
2 leaves fresh basil
1 sprig thyme
1 teaspoon pepper, fresh cracked
2 tablespoons Dijon mustard

In food processor, blend all ingredients thoroughly.
Add:
1 cup olive oil
½ cup rice vinegar
¼ cup honey
Salt to taste

Slowly add olive oil to form emulsion. Add vinegar and honey. Adjust seasonings, chill.

❧

TENDERLOIN EGGS BENEDICT
Serves 6

6 English muffins, split
12 3-ounce tenderloin medallions
12 poached eggs
2 cups Perfect Béarnaise Sauce

Top muffins with 2 tenderloins that have been sautéed (preferably grilled) to medium rare; top each with 2 poached eggs (eggs may be poached ahead of time, held in ice water, and reheated in hot water at time of service).

Ladle 1¼ ounces Béarnaise over top of eggs, serve immediately.

Accompany with Apple-Cinnamon Coffee Cake and Hashed Brown Potatoes and Cream (page 28).

PERFECT BÉARNAISE SAUCE
Serves 6

½ cup white wine vinegar
½ cup dry vermouth
2 tablespoons shallots, minced
1 teaspoon dried tarragon
½ teaspoon salt
½ teaspoon black pepper

Combine ingredients in a saucepan and reduce until almost no liquid remains, set aside.
To finish:
6 egg yolks
8 tablespoons unsalted butter, cold
1¼ cups unsalted butter, clarified, melted
6 to 7 drops hot pepper sauce
Salt to taste

Put egg yolks in a stainless bowl and whip vigorously for 1 minute. Add 4 tablespoons cold butter. Set the bowl over boiling water, whip continuously at a moderate pace until the yolks thicken and pan bottom can be seen between strokes. Remove at once, add remaining cold butter, a piece at a time. Slowly dribble the melted butter into the sauce while whisking. Add the tarragon reduction from the set-aside pan, blend. Add hot sauce, check for salt, stir.

Note: Broken (separated) sauce may be re-emulsified by placing a small amount of ice water in a bowl, and slowly dribbling in all the sauce while whisking.

HASHED BROWN POTATOES AND CREAM
Serves 6

1½ pounds fresh potatoes, shredded
4 spring onion tops, sliced
2 cups heavy cream
10 strips bacon, cooked, diced (thick smoked bacon is recommended)
Seasoning salt, to taste

Preheat oven to 350°.
Mix all ingredients in a mixing bowl. Pour into a buttered 10-inch baking pan, bake 45 minutes until golden brown.

❧

APPLE-CINNAMON COFFEE CAKE
Yield, 1 10-inch coffee cake

One:

1⅔ cups all-purpose flour
1⅔ cups sugar
⅞ cup quick rolled oats
⅞ cup butter, cold

Place ingredients in a mixing bowl, blend until butter is cut into dry ingredients to the size of a pea. Set aside ¼ cup of the mixture.

Two:

1¾ teaspoons baking powder
1 teaspoon cinnamon
¼ teaspoon salt
¼ teaspoon baking soda
¼ teaspoon nutmeg

Add to the mixing bowl, blend.

Three:

⅞ cup buttermilk
3 eggs
2 chopped apples

Blend together buttermilk and eggs, then add to mixing bowl, blend until just moist, add apples.
Preheat oven to 350°.
Pour mixture into a 10-inch greased baking pan. Bake for 30 minutes, or until done.

❧

CHOCOLATE PECAN PIE
Yield 1 10-inch pie

1½ cups sugar
1½ cups light corn syrup
3 whole eggs
3 tablespoons butter, melted
1 tablespoon vanilla extract
2 cups pecan halves
4 ounces semisweet chocolate, chopped
1 10-inch deep-dish pie shell

Preheat oven to 350°.
Mix first 5 ingredients until blended. Add pecans and chocolate, stir until blended, pour into pie shell. Bake for 40 to 50 minutes, until set. Remove from oven, cool. Serve refrigerated or at room temperature with Kentucky Bourbon Sauce.

KENTUCKY BOURBON SAUCE
Yield 2½ cups

1 cup heavy cream
1 cup half-and-half
4 egg yolks
½ cup sugar
2 tablespoons Kentucky bourbon, or to taste

Blend cream and half-and-half in a pan, bring to a boil, stirring. In a separate bowl, blend yolks and sugar until pale in color. Temper eggs with a bit of the hot milk, return mixture to the boiling milk, stirring constantly. Cook until the sauce coats the back of a spoon. Remove from heat, strain. Cool to room temperature. Add bourbon to taste. ❧

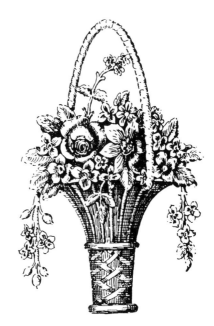

*E*NTERTAINING THE *V.I.P.*

Stouffer Mayflower Hotel
Washington, D.C.

*W*ashington is a city of power, elegance, and, of course, history. The Mayflower has been part of this milieu since 1925. Presidents and kings, barons of industry, political luminaries, and entertainment celebrities have all enjoyed the Mayflower, symbol of Washington hospitality.

Washington hosts a collection of fine dining establishments, yet few compare to the superb cuisine, elegant atmosphere, and long-established traditions of Nicholas, the Mayflower's signature restaurant. Displaying classic American styling, accented with sprays of fresh flowers, Nicholas offers the finest Mid-Atlantic and new American cuisine prepared by master chefs. For lunch or dinner, entertaining important business associates, or an intimate dinner with someone special, nothing surpasses Nicholas.

Smoked Salmon and Beluga Caviar Ravioli

Mayflower Lamb Chops
with Straw Potatoes, Red Pepper Sauce,
Spinach Timbale, and Ragout of Mushrooms

Napoleon of Fresh Berries

Almond Tuiles

COLOR PLATE 10

SMOKED SALMON AND BELUGA CAVIAR RAVIOLI
Serves 6

24 thin slices smoked salmon for ravioli
3 ounces Beluga caviar
12 slices smoked salmon to cover plate
2 eggs, hard boiled
2 whole lemons, wedge cut
1 onion, finely diced
6 sprigs dill

Cut the 24 slices of smoked salmon with a slicing knife on the bias. With a 2-inch cookie cutter, cut out 24 circles. Place 2 circles on each plate.

In center of circles place ½ ounce of Beluga caviar. Place the remaining salmon circles on top, folding back 1 side so that the caviar is visible.

Place 2 slices of salmon on each plate and garnish with separated chopped boiled egg yolks and whites, lemon wedges, diced onion, and a sprig of dill.

❧

MAYFLOWER LAMB CHOPS WITH STRAW POTATOES
Serves 6

18 single lamb chops
Salt and pepper
Cooking oil
Butter, melted
6 large potatoes

Preheat oven to 400°.

Season lamb chops with salt and pepper. Place in hot pan with a little oil and sear on both sides. Remove lamb chops from pan and brush with butter.

Clean and peel potatoes, cut into fine straw potatoes. Press potatoes to both sides of seared lamb chops and sauté on both sides until potatoes are crisp.

Place in oven for 5 minutes or until cooked. Serve with Red Pepper Sauce, Spinach Timbale, and Ragout of Mushrooms.

RED PEPPER SAUCE
Serves 6

⅓ cup butter
6 red peppers, seeded, rough chopped
½ onion, diced
3 shallots, chopped
2 cloves garlic, chopped
Salt and pepper

Heat butter, sauté together the red peppers, onion, shallots, and garlic. Season with salt and pepper. Sauté on low heat for 20 minutes.

Completely puree mixture, strain. Adjust seasonings to taste.

SPINACH TIMBALE
Serves 6

1 pound fresh spinach, cleaned
6 tablespoons butter
1 cup half-and-half
3 eggs
Salt and pepper

Preheat oven to 375°.

Sauté spinach in butter until cooked. Remove from pan and squeeze out excess juice until it is almost dry. Puree spinach in food processor adding the half-and-half and eggs. Salt and pepper to taste.

Pour into 4-ounce buttered soufflé molds and bake in water bath for approximately 15 minutes. Remove from water bath and unmold.

RAGOUT OF MUSHROOMS
Serves 6

8 ounces chanterelle mushrooms, halved
8 ounces white mushrooms, halved
6 shallots, finely chopped
½ cup unsalted butter
⅓ cup dry white wine
Salt and pepper

Sauté mushrooms and shallots in butter over low heat. Add dry white wine and reduce until evaporated. Salt and pepper to taste.

❧

NAPOLEON OF FRESH BERRIES
Serves 6

Almond Tuiles
1 pint vanilla ice cream
1 pint whipping cream
Fresh seasonal berries; 1 pint each raspberries, blackberries, blueberries
6 mint sprigs
Confectioners' sugar

Place 1 tuile on each plate. Spread ice cream on tuile leaving a small border. Pipe whip cream around ice cream in a full circle. Place berries on top of whipped cream.

Place another tuile on top and repeat same filling.

Place third tuile on top and pipe rosette of whipped cream in the center. Garnish with a spring of mint and confectioners' sugar. ❧

ALMOND TUILES
page 113

SUMMER

Fresh from the Bay

Cafe Majestic, at The Majestic Hotel
San Francisco, California

*J*ust off the lobby of the authentically restored Majestic Hotel, the Cafe Majestic blends contemporary vitality with Edwardian grandeur—light and airy during the day, elegant and romantic at night. Foam-green wainscot and apricot walls complement graceful columns, potted palms, and unusual cast-iron and oak chairs. Adjoining the restaurant is a 150-year-old bar (originally found in a Paris cafe), backed by mirrors and a striking collection of butterflies.

The cafe's chef, Matt Wyss, artfully creates California cuisine with strong Italian and Spanish accents. The Cafe Majestic—a symbol of the very best of San Francisco, voted "San Francisco's Most Romantic Restaurant" by *S.F. Focus Magazine* for four years—blends fine dining with beauty, charm, gracious living, and warm hospitality.

Shellfish Soup
with Fennel and Sweet Onions

Grilled Sturgeon
with Sauce Romesco

Huckleberry Herring

Black Pepper-Chocolate Cookies

COLOR PLATE II

SHELLFISH SOUP
WITH FENNEL AND SWEET ONIONS
Serves 6

Soup base:
½ cup olive oil
4 Vidalia or Maui onions, thinly sliced
2 medium fennel bulbs, thinly sliced
6 cloves garlic, peeled
2 bay leaves
3 sprigs fresh thyme, chopped
1 teaspoon chili pepper flakes, crushed
2 Roma tomatoes, peeled, seeded, diced

Heat the olive oil in an 8-quart Dutch oven over medium heat. Add the onions, fennel, garlic, bay leaves, thyme, and chili flakes. Lower heat, cook gently 30 minutes, stirring often. Add the tomatoes and cook an additional 15 minutes.

Shellfish:
¼ cup olive oil
1 yellow onion, quartered
2 bay leaves
2 teaspoons whole black peppercorns
2 pounds mussels, scrubbed, debearded
1 pound medium shrimp, shelled, deveined
2 pounds Manila or littleneck clams, scrubbed
2 cups white wine

Heat the olive oil in a pan large enough to hold the shellfish. Add the onion, bay leaves, and peppercorns, cook gently for 10 minutes. Add the mussels, shrimp, and clams. Raise the heat and cook 2 minutes, stirring constantly. Add the white wine and cover the pot. Steam until the mussels and clams open. Strain and reserve the cooking juices and shellfish.

To finish:
4 cups clam juice
Kosher salt
White pepper
¼ cup Italian parsley leaves, coarsely chopped

Add the juices from the shellfish to the pot of onions and fennel; add the clam juice and simmer soup for 10 minutes, skimming and discarding any foam that forms on top. Remove the clams and mussels from their shells and add them and the shrimp to the soup. Season with salt and white pepper to taste, add parsley just before serving.

GRILLED STURGEON
Serves 6

6 6-ounce sturgeon fillets
Kosher salt
Ground white pepper

Prepare a moderate mesquite or oak fire in an outdoor barbeque. When the coals have developed a white ash, place the grill over them and oil it to prevent the fish from sticking.

Season the fillets with salt and pepper and grill 1 side for 5 minutes, turn over and cook an additional 4 minutes.

Place fillets on serving plates and sauce generously with Sauce Romesco. Serve with an aromatic rice and grilled seasonal vegetables.

SAUCE ROMESCO
Serves 6

2 dried Ancho chili peppers, seeded, stemmed
1 dried red Japanese chili pepper, seeded
1 cup water
½ cup sherry vinegar
1 cup extra virgin olive oil
2½ slices French bread, ¼-inch thick
2 large tomatoes, peeled, chopped
2 tablespoons almonds, sliced, toasted
2 tablespoons hazelnuts, peeled, toasted
6 cloves garlic, peeled, chopped
Kosher salt

Place peppers in a saucepan with the water and vinegar. Bring mixture to a rapid boil over a high flame, reduce heat, simmer 5 minutes. Remove the peppers from the water and cool, reserving water.

In ⅓ cup olive oil, fry the bread slices on both sides until golden brown. Remove the bread from the pan and fry the tomatoes in the same oil for 3 minutes. Reserve the oil.

Combine all ingredients including the reserved oil (excluding water and salt) in the work bowl of a food processor and chop until well blended but retaining texture. Adjust consistency with reserved water until it pours off a spoon like catsup. Salt to taste.

HUCKLEBERRY HERRING
Serves 6

1 pint good quality vodka
½ pound sugar
1 pound fresh huckleberries

Combine the vodka and sugar in a 2-quart bottle. Stir or shake well until the sugar is dissolved. Add the huckleberries and cover tightly. Shake well, refrigerate for 30 days. Strain. Serve with Black Pepper-Chocolate Cookies.

BLACK PEPPER-CHOCOLATE COOKIES
Yield, 3 dozen cookies

¾ cup butter
1 cup sugar
1 large egg
1½ cups all-purpose flour
⅓ cup cocoa
⅛ teaspoon salt
1 teaspoon freshly ground pepper
¼ teaspoon cayenne pepper
½ teaspoon ground cinnamon

Cream together the butter and sugar with a mixer at medium speed. When the mixture is fluffy, add the egg and blend well with the mixer on high. Sift together the remaining ingredients and add to the mixture. Mix thoroughly until a firm dough is formed. Cover and chill for 1 hour.

Preheat oven to 350°.

Roll out the dough to a thickness of ⅛ inch on a lightly floured surface. Cut into 1-inch rounds and bake for 10 minutes. ✎

BY THE BEACH

The Don CeSar — a Registry Resort
St. Petersburg Beach, Florida

Built in 1928 at the height of the Jazz Era by a romantic who named it after the hero of his favorite opera, this historic pink "castle" on Florida's west coast evokes the feel and flavor of Europe. French marble fountains, antique candelabras, Italian crystal chandeliers, and exquisite works of art complement the high ceilings and tall windows of the hotel's Mediterranean and Moorish architecture.

Set on an island in the Gulf of Mexico, The Don CeSar offers numerous beachfront pleasures from swimming to scuba diving and tennis to golf. But one's visit is equally remembered for the resort's award-winning kitchens, whose talented chefs highlight the region's diverse selection of seafood and fresh produce in traditional dishes with a contemporary flair.

Florida Lobster Salad

Mesquite-Smoked Grouper

Tea-Smoked Shrimp
with Peanuts and Cucumber Sauce

Grand Marnier Duck
with Honey Soy Glaze,
Sweet Potato Cakes, and Orange Herb Dressing

Burgundy Poached Pears
with Cinnamon Ice Cream and Caramel Sauce

COLOR PLATE 12

FLORIDA LOBSTER SALAD
Serves 4

2 to 3 Florida lobster tails (shrimp or crab may be substituted)
1 orange, sectioned, juice reserved
1 pink or ruby grapefruit, sectioned, juice reserved
1 carambola (starfruit), sliced
1 small mango, diced
1 large red pepper, roasted, skinned, seeded, diced
1 avocado, diced
½ red onion, thinly sliced
2 tablespoons lemon juice
2 tablespoons lime juice
½ cup olive oil
2 tablespoons fresh herbs (dill, parsley, basil), chopped
1 scant teaspoon fresh chilis, minced
1 teaspoon fresh ginger, grated
½ teaspoon sesame oil
¼ teaspoon salt
2 cups mixed fresh greens
Black sesame seeds

Simmer lobster in a court bouillon until fully cooked, about 5 minutes. Remove meat from shell and cool. Dice into large chunks and toss with orange, grapefruit, starfruit, mango, red pepper, avocado, and red onion.

Mix all juices and olive oil with fresh herbs, chilis, ginger, sesame oil, and salt. Toss with lobster and fruits.

Serve on a bed of mixed greens, sprinkle with black sesame seeds. Seaweed makes a nice garnish.

❧

MESQUITE-SMOKED GROUPER
Serves 4

¼ cup brown sugar
1 tablespoon Worcestershire sauce
2 tablespoons lime juice
⅓ cup whole seed or whole-grain mustard
⅓ cup jalapeño jelly
¼ cup white wine
¼ cup olive oil
1 tablespoon barbeque spice mix
4 6- to 8-ounce grouper fillets (salmon or other firm fish may be substituted)
Mesquite chips

Mix all marinade ingredients thoroughly. Place fillets in marinade, cover, let stand several hours.

Soak the mesquite chips in water. Prepare charcoal. When the coals have turned white, add the drained mesquite chips to begin smoking. Allow 2 to 3 minutes before placing fish on the grill.

Remove fish from marinade, place on grill, cover and let smoke, turning to avoid burning; baste with marinade. Approximate cooking time is 10 to 12 minutes.

Serve with a fresh fruit or tomato salsa.

TEA-SMOKED SHRIMP
WITH PEANUTS AND CUCUMBER SAUCE
Serves 6 to 8

36   16/20-count jumbo shrimp
2 tablespoons Chinese black tea leaves
1 tablespoon peanut oil
1 tablespoon cilantro, chopped
½ teaspoon oriental chili paste
1 tablespoon fresh ginger, grated
2 tablespoons honey
½ cup soy sauce
½ cup sake
2 tablespoons lime or lemon juice
1 tablespoon sesame oil
½ teaspoon Chinese five spice powder
Roasted peanuts

Peel and devein shrimp. Marinate in a mixture of all ingredients (except tea leaves and peanut oil) for 20 minutes.

Set up a smoker on top of stove by using a large roasting pan with wire rack and cover. Lay shrimp on rack and baste with marinade. Heat pan, add oil, then sprinkle in the tea leaves. Cover tightly and allow to smoke until the shrimp are tender, but not overcooked, 3 to 5 minutes.

Shrimp may be served immediately or allowed to cool.

Present on a platter with Cucumber Sauce and roasted peanuts. Garnish with cilantro, sliced cucumbers, mint, or fried rice noodles, if desired. Serve with warm sake, ice cold beer, champagne, or dry white wine.

CUCUMBER SAUCE
Yield, 2½ cups

6 tablespoons rice vinegar
3 cucumbers, lightly peeled, seeded
½ teaspoon sesame oil
¼ cup olive oil
1 teaspoon salt
¼ teaspoon white pepper
1 teaspoon sugar

Place the rice vinegar in a blender. Dice the cucumbers and add in batches, puree until very smooth. Add the remaining ingredients and adjust to taste.

Refrigerate until ready to use.

GRAND MARNIER DUCK
Serves 6 to 8

4 4- to 5-pound Long Island (Peking) ducks, breasts
  removed without bone, legs removed, hip bone
  removed, fat trimmed
1 cup Grand Marnier (triple sec may be substituted)
2 tablespoons Cajun seasoning or Chinese five spice
  powder
6 cloves garlic, chopped
3 bay leaves
1 tablespoon black pepper, coarse ground
1 teaspoon fresh or dried rosemary
1 teaspoon fresh or dried thyme
1 tablespoon fresh ginger, grated
1 tablespoon sesame oil

*Marinate duck in all ingredients for 4 to 6 hours.
Drain and allow to dry before cooking.*

*Prepare a charcoal grill and cook duck legs over
moderate heat, turning frequently. When legs are fully
cooked, place duck breasts on grill and cook for about 5
minutes, until medium rare. Brush with Honey Soy
Glaze, turn and baste until golden. Keep warm until
ready to serve. At serving time, coat duck with Orange
Herb Dressing, serve with Sweet Potato Cakes.*

HONEY SOY GLAZE
Yield, 1 cup

Blend:
½ cup honey
½ cup soy sauce
1 teaspoon fresh ginger, grated
½ teaspoon sesame oil

SWEET POTATO CAKES
Serves 6 to 8

4 to 5 large sweet potatoes or yams
½ cup onion, finely minced
2 large eggs
2 heaping tablespoons parsley, chopped
2 heaping tablespoons chives, chopped
½ cup all-purpose flour
½ teaspoon white pepper
1 teaspoon salt
Oil, for cooking

Preheat oven to 300º.

*Finely grate sweet potatoes into a bowl and mix with
other ingredients. Heat some vegetable oil in a fry pan
until hot. Form sweet potato mixture into patties 3 inches
in diameter, brown on both sides. Place browned patties
in oven for 5 minutes until fully cooked. Keep warmed
until ready to serve.*

ORANGE HERB DRESSING
Yield, 2½ cups

2 seedless oranges
1 cup orange juice
1 cup olive oil
¼ cup lemon juice
¼ cup white wine vinegar or rice vinegar
¼ teaspoon salt
⅛ teaspoon white pepper
2 tablespoons basil, chopped
1 tablespoon parsley, chopped
1 teaspoon fresh rosemary or cilantro
2 green onions, chopped

*Grate the zest from the oranges, reserve. Remove the
peel with a sharp knife and dice the flesh fine. Mix the
orange with all the other ingredients except the herbs. At
serving time, add herbs and stir.*

BURGUNDY POACHED PEARS
WITH CINNAMON ICE CREAM AND CARAMEL SAUCE
Serves 8

8 Bosc, Anjou, or Bartlett pears, ripe but not soft
3 cups burgundy (or any red wine)
1 cup water
1 cinnamon stick
½ cup granulated sugar
1 quart cinnamon ice cream (or use vanilla ice cream and
  add cinnamon to caramel sauce)
¼ cup brown sugar
½ cup dark chocolate shavings
8 mint sprigs

*Peel pears leaving natural shape intact. Leave stem
attached, core from the bottom, remove seeds. Place in a
sauce pan and add wine, water, cinnamon, and sugar —
the pears must be covered by the liquid. Bring to a boil
and simmer 15 minutes until fork tender, taking care not
to overcook. Allow to cool in the liquid. This may be done
1 day in advance of serving and stored in the liquid.*

*To serve, have 8 plates in freezer. Warm pears slightly.
Prescoop the ice cream (2 per serving) and have it ready
in the freezer. Place pear on the plate with ice cream in
front. Sprinkle entire plate and rim with brown sugar
and chocolate shavings. Use a spoon to drizzle Caramel
Sauce over the entire plate and garnish with mint.* ❧

CARAMEL SAUCE
page 119

An Evening for Gourmets

The Greenbrier
White Sulphur Springs, West Virginia

Throughout the 19th century, The Greenbrier was *the* Southern summer resort. Guests came to use the mineral water, to enjoy the mountain climate, and to mingle with the famous of the day. Today, many of the original cottages are preserved as guest accommodations, although enlarged and modernized. In 1913, The Greenbrier opened on a year-round basis, with golf and tennis as featured attractions. One of The Greenbrier's most endearing qualities, certainly, is its ability to have retained the best of the past for the pleasure of the present. For generations, visitors have enjoyed The Greenbrier's seclusion and the healing powers of the legendary waters, complemented by the finest in facilities and superb cuisine.

Pan-Seared Atlantic White Salmon
on Bay Scallop Cream with Fresh Herbs and Trout Caviar

Raspberry and Fresh Thyme Sorbet

Greenbrier Valley Lamb Mixed Grill
Petit Lamb Chop, Roasted Loin, and Chipolata,
with Printanier Vegetables and Rosti Potato

Early Spring Greens
with Roasted Garlic Caesar Dressing

Chocolate Mocha Torte
with Fresh Lemon Curd

COLOR PLATE 13

Continued, page 39

COLOR PLATE 9   A BRUNCH WITH FRIENDS   PAGE 26
The Saint Paul Hotel

L/R: Chocolate Pecan Pie, Tenderloin Eggs Benedict, Hashed Brown Potatoes and Cream,
Apple-Cinnamon Coffee Cake, Seasonal Fruits with Devonshire Cream, Grilled Tuna Salad

Photography: Kanji Takeno

COLOR PLATE 10   ENTERTAINING THE V.I.P.   PAGE 29
Stouffer Mayflower Hotel

L/R: Napoleon of Fresh Berries, Lamb Chops with Straw Potatoes and Red Pepper Sauce,
Spinach Timbale, Ragout of Mushrooms, Smoked Salmon and Beluga Caviar Ravioli

FRESH FROM THE BAY
Cafe Majestic, at The Majestic Hotel

Grilled Sturgeon with Sauce Romesco

COLOR PLATE 12

BY THE BEACH
The Don CeSar, a Registry Resort

PAGE 35

Mesquite Smoked Grouper

PAN-SEARED ATLANTIC WHITE SALMON
Serves 6

6 2-ounce pieces Atlantic white salmon, skin on
1 tablespoon extra virgin olive oil
2 tablespoons parsley, chopped
Salt and pepper

Coat salmon with olive oil, parsley, salt and pepper to taste, and marinate 2 hours.

Sear the salmon, skin-side down, in a nonstick pan until the skin is crispy. Turn and sear the other side. (Thick fillets may need to be finished in a 375° oven for 3 to 4 minutes.) Serve with Bay Scallop Cream.

BAY SCALLOP CREAM
Serves 6

1 teaspoon extra virgin olive oil
1 shallot, sliced
2 tablespoons celery, sliced
2 tablespoons onion, sliced
2 tablespoons leek, sliced
1 bay leaf
1 sprig fresh thyme
6 black peppercorns
1½ cups fish stock
1 cup dry white wine
1 cup fresh bay scallops
1½ cups cream reduced to 1 cup
1 tablespoon unsalted butter
1 tablespoon fresh dill sprigs
1 tablespoon fresh cilantro sprigs
1 tablespoon fresh chives, cut ½-inch long
2 tablespoons fresh trout caviar

In 1-quart saucepan, heat the olive oil and sweat the vegetables, bay leaf, thyme, and peppercorns until soft, about 2 minutes. Add ¾ cup fish stock and ½ cup wine and simmer to reduce. In another pan bring the remaining stock and wine to a simmer and poach the scallops until they are just cooked, 1 to 2 minutes.

Pour ½ the poaching liquid into the simmering stock and reduce to ⅓ its volume. Put the scallops and remaining poaching liquid in a blender with the cream, and fine puree; strain. Put the scallop cream in a saucepan and reduce by ½. Strain the reduced stock into the cream sauce and whisk in the butter until emulsified. Adjust seasonings. Gently fold in the fresh herbs and trout caviar just before serving.

RASPBERRY AND FRESH THYME SORBET
page 113

GREENBRIER VALLEY LAMB MIXED GRILL
Serves 6

6 2-ounce single bone lamb chops
1 7-ounce boneless lamb loin
1 tablespoon fresh rosemary, chopped
2 cloves garlic, minced
3 tablespoons olive oil
Salt and freshly ground black pepper
6 1-ounce chipolata (spicy lamb sausages)

Rub the lamb chops and loin with the rosemary, garlic, and olive oil, season with salt and pepper. Marinate 2 hours.

Blanch sausages in simmering water for 4 minutes, cool and reserve.

Preheat oven to 400°.

To serve, grill the lamb chops on a broiler until medium rare. Sear both sides of loin in a skillet, transfer to the oven and roast until medium rare (reserve the skillet drippings for cooking vegetables, following). Sear the sausages in a heavy skillet until golden brown. Place 1 chop, 1 slice loin, and 1 chipolata on each plate.

Serve with Printanier Vegetables and Rosti Potatoes.

PRINTANIER VEGETABLES
Serves 6

1 pound asparagus tips, peeled
1 cup turnips, diced
1 cup fresh green peas
1½ dozen baby carrots, peeled, split
1 cup fresh pearl onions
½ pound unsalted butter, melted
Salt and freshly ground black pepper

Blanch and cool all vegetables separately. At service, reheat the vegetables, except onions, by simmering in water; drain, toss in butter until lightly coated. Salt and pepper to taste.

Cook the pearl onions until golden brown in the reserved lamb skillet.

ROSTI POTATOES
Serves 6

2 large Idaho potatoes
Salt and freshly ground black pepper
Clarified butter

Bake the potatoes until they are ¾ done, cool.

Peel and shred the potatoes, salt and pepper to taste. Heat some clarified butter in 3-inch skillet, add a layer of potatoes and sauté until a nice golden crust is formed on both sides. To serve, cut in half.

EARLY SPRING GREENS
Serves 6

1 bunch each mazuna, arugula, red oak lettuce,
  sunflower sprouts, and mâche

*Clean and trim greens, chill in ice water until ready
to use. Serve with Roasted Garlic Caesar Dressing.*

ROASTED GARLIC CAESAR DRESSING
Yield, about 1¼ cups

1 egg yolk
2 tablespoons lemon juice
2 anchovy fillets, drained, chopped
1 clove garlic, finely minced
5 cloves garlic, roasted in skins
1 teaspoon Worcestershire sauce
½ teaspoon black pepper, coarsely ground
1 tablespoon white wine
1 cup extra virgin olive oil
2 tablespoons Parmesan cheese, freshly grated
1 teaspoon parsley, chopped

*In a blender or food processor, whisk egg, lemon juice,
and anchovy until frothy. Add the minced garlic, roasted
garlic pulp (squeezed from skins), Worcestershire, pepper,
and wine. Blend until smooth.*

*With blender running, add the olive oil slowly until
mixture is emulsified. Fold in Parmesan and parsley.
Adjust seasonings.*

CHOCOLATE MOCHA TORTE
Serves 12

Pecan layer:
2½ cups pecan pieces
½ cup granulated sugar
¼ teaspoon salt
½ cup unsalted butter, melted, cooled

*Position a rack in the top of the oven and preheat to
350°.*

*Lightly butter the bottom and sides of a 10-inch
springform pan, line bottom of the pan with parchment
paper, butter the paper generously. Use a food processor
with metal blade to process pecans, sugar, and salt until
finely chopped. In a medium bowl, combine the pecan
mixture with the melted butter. Press the mixture firmly
and evenly into the bottom of the prepared pan. Freeze
the layer for 10 minutes, until quite cold. Bake for 15
minutes or until the edges begin to brown. Cool completely in pan on a wire rack. Cover with plastic wrap,
chill 1 hour until cold and firm.*

Chocolate fudge layer:
1¾ cups (½ pound) semisweet chocolate, finely chopped
1 cup heavy cream
4 tablespoons unsalted butter, softened
2 tablespoons light corn syrup

*Melt the chocolate with the cream in a double boiler,
stirring often. Remove from heat and stir in the butter
until smooth. Stir in the corn syrup. Transfer the mixture
to a medium bowl. Cool bowl in an ice bath until mixture begins to thicken.*

*Using a spatula, spread the fudge over the refrigerated
pecan layer. Cover the pan with plastic wrap and chill for
1 hour, until firm.*

Mocha layer:
½ cup semisweet chocolate, finely chopped
2 teaspoons instant coffee
4 large eggs at room temperature
1½ cups light brown sugar, packed
1 cup unsalted butter, softened

*Use a double boiler to melt the chocolate with the
instant coffee, stirring often until smooth; remove from
heat. Use a hand-held electric mixer at medium speed to
incorporate the eggs 1 at a time. Add the brown sugar and
mix for 1 minute until fluffy and light. Gradually beat in
the butter. Remove the plastic wrap from the springform
pan. Spread the mocha layer evenly over the fudge layer.
Cover the surface with plastic wrap and freeze 1 hour,
until very firm.*

Japonaise layer:
1½ cups (5 ounces) hazelnut (filbert) flour
2¼ tablespoons all-purpose flour
1⅓ cups granulated sugar
¾ cup egg whites

Preheat oven to 215°.

*In a stainless steel bowl, mix the flours and all but ½
cup of the sugar. Beat the egg whites with remaining
sugar into a meringue, fold in the flour mixture in thirds.
Pipe out the meringue in 2⅜-inch circles on parchment
paper and bake for approximately 1 to 2 hours, until dry.
Reserve in a dry place.*

Frosting:
3 cups heavy cream, divided
2 tablespoons instant coffee
¾ cup confectioners' sugar

*In a small saucepan over low heat, warm 1 cup cream
with the instant coffee, stirring until the coffee dissolves.
Transfer to a bowl, chill over ice until very cold. In a
chilled bowl, beat the remaining cream with the cooled
coffee cream and confectioners' sugar until stiff enough to
hold its form when cut with a knife.*

To assemble:
*Remove the torte from the freezer and uncover. Use a
thin-bladed knife to cut around edge of the torte to loosen
from the pan. Rest the cake gently on its side, use the knife
to separate the cake from the pan bottom, remove parchment paper. Place torte, pecan layer down, on an inverted
10-inch cake pan. Cut 12 2⅜-inch circles with a pastry
cutter. Return them to the freezer.*

*When assembling, add the frosting to tops of the circles
with a plain-tipped pastry bag. Top each with the reserved
japonaise. Serve with fresh Lemon Curd (page 113).* ❧

On the Fourth of July

The Hay-Adams Hotel
Washington, D.C.

Since 1927, The Hay-Adams has played host to the world's powerful and influential. The hotel is today the only privately held property on Lafayette Square, and commands a superb view of the White House. Just steps from the Mall and all of its July 4th activity, the hotel has been a favorite stop for Independence Day visitors for generations. Here is a menu for an afternoon of picnicking and an evening of fireworks.

Start the event with favorite appetizers, tasty tidbits, and snacks. Continue with the two salads, topped off with a delightful Patriotic Fruit Tart. When you return home from the festivities, finish the day with a chilled glass of milk and a sampling of the crunchy cookies that have baked to perfection while you were away.

Chicken and Pepper Salad
with Maple Vinaigrette Dressing

Shrimp and Two Cabbage Slaw

A Patriotic Fruit Tart

While-You-Were-Away Cookies

COLOR PLATE 14

Chicken and Pepper Salad with Maple Vinaigrette Dressing
Serves 6 to 8

6 to 8 boneless chicken breasts, skin removed
¾ cup olive oil
2 lemons, juiced
2 tablespoons maple syrup
1 red bell pepper, ½-inch diced
1 yellow bell pepper, ½-inch diced
6 spring onions, thin-diagonal cut
1 tablespoon prepared mustard
Salt and fresh ground pepper to taste

Sauté the chicken breasts in a hot pan with a couple teaspoons of the olive oil, taking care not to overly brown; remove from pan. While still warm, dice the chicken into ½-inch pieces. In a bowl, dress the chicken with the juice of 1 lemon, 1 tablespoon maple syrup, and 2 teaspoons olive oil; allow to cool completely (the chicken will absorb the dressing). Add the peppers and onions to the chicken.

For balance of the dressing, mix the mustard with the remaining maple syrup and lemon juice. Whisk while slowly adding the olive oil (the dressing will be thick). Season to taste with salt and pepper. If the dressing is too sweet, add lemon juice; if too sour, add maple syrup.

Fold the dressing into the salad. For best flavor, refrigerate for 2 hours before serving.

❧

Shrimp and Two Cabbage Slaw
Serves 6

1 pound shrimp, cooked, peeled, deveined
½ small head white cabbage
½ small head red cabbage
1 large ripe tomato, seeded, ½-inch cubed
1 egg yolk
2 teaspoons prepared mustard
1 tablespoon balsamic vinegar
1 cup olive oil
2 teaspoons prepared horseradish
Shrimp seasoning, salt and pepper

Select shrimp to a size of your liking. Cut cabbage halves again in half, thinly slice, place in a bowl. Add cubed tomato and shrimp.

To prepare the mayonnaise dressing, place the egg yolk in the bowl with the mustard and vinegar, mix. While whisking, slowly add the oil. The yolk should accommodate ¾ to 1 cup oil. Add horseradish, season the dressing with shrimp seasoning, salt and pepper if needed. Fold the dressing into the salad. Use a few reserved shrimp to decorate the top of the salad.

❧

A Patriotic Fruit Tart
Yield, 1 10-inch tart

Crust:
2 cups flour
¼ cup sugar
½ teaspoon salt
⅔ cup shortening or butter
⅔ cup water

Mix the flour, sugar, and salt. Cut the shortening into the flour mixture with a pastry cutter, leaving the fat in pea-sized pieces. Mix with the water and form into a ball. Let the dough rest in the refrigerator for ½ hour.

Filling:
5 to 6 Granny Smith apples, peeled, cored, sliced
1 cup cranberries, fresh or frozen
½ cup fresh blueberries
½ cup each of flour and sugar
2 teaspoons cinnamon
¼ teaspoon salt
1 pint whipping cream
Confectioners' sugar

Preheat oven to 350°.

Roll out ¾ of the dough about ¼-inch thick; line a 10-inch tart pan with ½ of the dough.

Mix the apples with the cranberries and blueberries in the unbaked shell. Mix the flour, sugar, cinnamon, and salt, sprinkle over the fruit.

Roll out the balance of the dough, form into a lattice and place over the fruit.

Bake until the fruit is bubbling between the lattice and pastry sightly browns, about 30 to 45 minutes.

While the tart bakes, whip the cream with a bit of confectioners' sugar for sweetness. When the tart is done, serve with rosettes of whipped cream, garnish with fresh blueberries, if desired.

❧

While-You-Were-Away Cookies
Yield, 2 dozen

2 egg whites
⅔ cup sugar
Pinch salt
⅛ teaspoon cream of tartar
1 teaspoon vanilla extract
1 cup chocolate or butterscotch chips
1 cup pecans, chopped

Preheat oven to 400°.

Line a cookie sheet with aluminium foil. Whip the egg whites until they begin to froth, slowly add the sugar, salt, and cream of tartar. Finish whipping into stiff peaks. Gently fold in the vanilla, chips, and pecans.

Place mounded teaspoonfuls of the mixture about 1 inch apart on the foil-lined sheet. Put the cookie sheet in the oven and turn the oven off. Leave the cookies in the oven for 6 to 8 hours, until completely dry and crisp. ❧

An Antebellum Afternoon

John Rutledge House Inn /King's Courtyard Inn
Charleston, South Carolina

A National Historic Landmark, the John Rutledge House was built in 1763 by John Rutledge, a noted signer of the U.S. Constitution. The inn incorporates two carriage houses plus the distinctive home. Restoration has enhanced the graceful ironwork and original elaborate interiors, which include carved Italian marble fireplaces and inlaid floors.

Its sister hotel, the antebellum King's Courtyard Inn is designed in the Greek Revival style with unusual Egyptian detailing. Built in 1853, it is one of King Street's oldest buildings. In its 139-year history it has housed shops, private residences, and an inn catering to plantation owners, shipping interests, and merchant guests.

Both inns combine the finest in historic surroundings with the benefit of all modern comforts and conveniences. What better hosts could there be to offer you a light, refreshing menu for casual entertaining?

Charleston Crab Dip

Shrimp Paste

Cucumber Sandwiches

Lemon Bars Deluxe

Plantation Punch

COLOR PLATE 15

CHARLESTON CRAB DIP
Yield, approximately 2½ cups

½ pound fresh crabmeat, cleaned
¾ cup New York sharp cheese, shredded
½ cup mayonnaise
¼ cup prepared horseradish
Tabasco
Fresh lemon juice
Worcestershire sauce
Seasoned salt

Combine crabmeat and cheese. Mix in mayonnaise and horseradish. Add remaining ingredients to taste, blend thoroughly, refrigerate. Flavors are best if it is allowed to sit 24 hours before serving.

SHRIMP PASTE
Yield, approximately 2 cups

8 ounces cream cheese
1 tablespoon fresh lemon juice
¼ teaspoon onion powder
Dash Tabasco
Pinch garlic salt
1 cup cooked shrimp, finely chopped
White bread, crusts trimmed
Pimento garnish

Soften cream cheese and blend in seasonings; blend mixture into cooked shrimp.
Cut bread slices at a diagonal to form triangles, trim crusts. Spread with shrimp paste, garnish with pimento.

CUCUMBER SANDWICHES
Yield, 3 dozen

8 ounces cream cheese
Mayonnaise
¼ teaspoon garlic powder
¼ teaspoon onion salt
Dash Worcestershire sauce
1 medium cucumber
Vinegar water
Loaf white bread
Olive slices or paprika, for garnish

Soften cream cheese, mix in just enough mayonnaise to make the mixture smooth. Blend in garlic powder, onion salt, and Worcestershire.
Score sides of cucumber with a fork. Slice thin, soak slices in mix of 1 part vinegar and 2 parts water.
Cut bread slices into 2-inch rounds, spread with cream cheese mixture. Top with a cucumber slice before serving. Garnish with olive slice or sprinkle with paprika.

LEMON BARS DELUXE
Yield, 36 bars

2¼ cups flour, divided
½ cup confectioners' sugar
1 cup butter, softened
4 eggs, beaten
2 cups sugar
⅓ cup lemon juice
½ teaspoon baking powder

Preheat oven to 350°.
Sift together 2 cups flour and ½ cup confectioners' sugar. Cut butter into mixture until it clings together sufficiently to be pressed into a greased 13 x 9 x 2-inch pan. Bake for 25 to 30 minutes or until lightly browned.
Combine eggs, sugar, and lemon juice, beat well. Sift together ¼ cup flour and baking powder, stir into egg mixture. Pour over baked crust. Bake an additional 25 to 30 minutes or until lightly browned. Sprinkle lightly with confectioners' sugar, cool, cut into bars.

PLANTATION PUNCH
Yield, approximately 1 gallon

1 fresh pineapple, cleaned and crushed, or 1 can prepared crushed pineapple, including juices
3 quarts orange juice
10 fresh lemons, squeezed
Grenadine, enough to color punch to desired shade
Rum, to taste
Fresh slices of oranges and lemons, and fresh mint leaves, for garnish

Mix all ingredients, serve over ice.

DIVING IN THE KEYS

La Concha, a Holiday Inn Hotel
Key West, Florida

Key West, surrounded by the warm, clear waters of the Gulf of Mexico and the Atlantic Ocean, is home to North America's only living coral reef. At home in these waters is a wide variety of sea life, ranging from the sailfish immortalized by Ernest Hemingway in *The Old Man and the Sea*, to the vividly colored yellowtail snapper, to the strangely built Florida lobster.

Considering the beauty and variety of sea life, it is no wonder that scuba and fishing enthusiasts from all over the world flock to Key West and, while on the island, that their choice for dining is the Holiday Inn La Concha. Chef Roger Hopkins of the landmark hotel is famous for turning these fabulous sea treasures into some very creative dishes.

Key West Seafood Fajita
Yellowtail "Cayo Hueso"
Lobster-Stuffed Chicken au Grand Marnier
Key Lime Pie
Key West Margaritas

COLOR PLATE 16

Key West Seafood Fajitas
Serves 4 to 6

2 ounces fresh yellowtail*
2 ounces fresh grouper*
2 ounces fresh shrimp, shells removed
2 ounces fresh tuna
1 each green, red, and yellow bell peppers
1 small red onion
2 tablespoons basil
¼ cup olive oil
2 tablespoons garlic, chopped
1 cup white wine
2 tablespoons powdered seafood seasoning
Salt and pepper to taste
*Any mild saltwater fish such as flounder, snapper, or
bluefish may be substituted

To serve:
½ cup salsa
½ cup guacamole
⅓ cup sour cream
½ cup cheddar cheese, grated
8 6-inch flour tortilla shells

Julienne all seafood and vegetables. Heat olive oil and
garlic in a sauté pan, when hot, add seafood; when
cooking, add white wine. Cook until seafood is nearly
done (2 to 4 minutes), add all remaining ingredients,
simmering until vegetables are semicrisp.

Preheat oven to 350°.

On a side dish, arrange salsa, guacamole, sour cream,
and cheese. Wrap tortillas in a moistened towel, heat in
oven for 3 to 4 minutes. Place hot seafood mixture on
tortilla shells, add above ingredients to each shell. Fold
into pocket shape, serve.

Yellowtail "Cayo Hueso"
Serves 4 to 6

½ cup flour
¼ cup coconut, shredded
4 7-ounce yellowtail snapper fillets (fresh saltwater
  flounder or any mild saltwater fish may be substituted)
¼ cup olive oil
2 tablespoons garlic, chopped
1 each red, green, and yellow bell peppers
1 small red onion
1 cup pineapple juice
2 cups white wine
1 tablespoon curry powder
Salt and pepper to taste
2 green bananas
2 tomatoes, wedge cut

Mix flour with ½ of the coconut. Dredge the fillets in
the mixture. Heat olive oil and chopped garlic in a sauté
pan. Lightly sauté each fillet until golden brown, remove
from pan, cover to keep warm.

Julienne bell peppers and onion, add to sauté pan,
cook until just crisp. Add pineapple juice, wine, and
seasonings, simmer 15 minutes. Slice green bananas into
ovals and add to the cooked vegetables. Add tomatoes,
simmer just until bananas are warmed.

Place fillets on individual plates. Spoon vegetable
sauce diagonally across each. Garnish with the warmed
bananas and tomatoes; sprinkle with remaining coconut.

LOBSTER-STUFFED CHICKEN AU GRAND MARNIER
Serves 4

4 chicken breasts, boned, skin removed
1 cup Key West Mojo sauce*
4 Florida lobster tails, removed from shell
2 tablespoons fresh garlic, chopped, mixed
  with 2 teaspoons olive oil
Salt and pepper
½ cup white wine
2 teaspoons butter
2 tablespoons lemon juice
Paprika

Cream sauce:
1 cup heavy cream
¼ cup Grand Marnier
2 teaspoons Parmesan cheese, freshly grated

Pound chicken breasts until flat, marinate for ½ hour in Mojo Sauce. Roll lobster tails in garlic and olive oil mixture, season with salt and pepper.

Preheat oven to 350°.

Place 1 lobster tail on the short end of each chicken breast and roll tightly. Place chicken/lobster rolls in a roasting pan, pour wine over the rolls. Dot each with butter, season with salt and pepper, sprinkle with lemon juice and dust with paprika. Roast for 20 to 25 minutes. Each roll should be firm to the touch.

Remove from the oven and keep warm.

To prepare cream sauce, place juices from roaster in a sauté pan. Bring to boil over high heat. Add heavy cream, cooking to reduce liquid to ¾ cup. Remove from heat.

Flame the Grand Marnier in an ovenproof cup and stir into the sauce. Add cheese. Spoon sauce onto serving plates, reserving a few tablespoons. Slice chicken/lobster rolls diagonally and fan open, place atop the sauce on the plates. Top each roll with remaining sauce.

*Mojo (pronounced Mo-Ho) sauce is a special blend of Caribbean herbs and spices, thus, no substitution is recommended. Your grocer may special order "Mojo Criollo," or you may write to: Nellie and Joe's, P.O. Box 2368, Key West, FL 33045.

KEY LIME PIE
Yield, 1 9-inch pie

Pie shell:
2 cups graham cracker crumbs
¼ pound butter
2 tablespoons sugar

Preheat oven to 350°.
Blend ingredients well, press into 9-inch pie plate. Bake 8 to 10 minutes, until lightly browned. Reduce oven setting to 250°.

Filling:
2 whole eggs
4 egg yolks
1 14-ounce can sweetened condensed milk
½ cup Key lime juice (add more for a tarter filling)

Mix thoroughly, pour into prebaked pie shell; bake at 250° for 5 minutes, remove from oven. Reset oven to 350°.

Meringue:
4 egg whites
2 tablespoons confectioners' sugar

Whip egg whites and sugar until stiff peaks form. Spread meringue on prebaked pie, working from outside rim to center to ensure that meringue seals to pie plate. Bake at 350° for 3 to 5 minutes, until the meringue is golden brown. Chill thoroughly before serving.

KEY WEST MARGARITAS
Serves 8

1 cup tequila
⅓ cup triple sec
1½ cups Key lime juice, freshly squeezed (or any lime
  juice or margarita mixer)
Salt, for glasses
Key lime slices, for garnish

Pour liquids into a large pitcher filled with ice, mix well.

Salt rims of 8 margarita glasses. Pour in margarita and garnish with Key lime slice.

Ingredients may be altered to suit individual tastes. Additional triple sec or a splash of lemon-lime soda will create sweeter margaritas. This recipe also works well blended and served frozen.

AFTER THE REGATTA

L'étoile, at The Charlotte Inn
Edgartown, Massachusetts

A glass-enclosed patio decorated with antiques and paintings, with French doors opening to a dining area in a beautiful outdoor garden, l'étoile is a perfect complement to Martha's Vineyard's famed Charlotte Inn, a stylish collection of five buildings, the oldest of which dates to 1705.

L'étoile was established in May of 1986 by Chef Michael Brisson and partner Joan Parzanese, whose use of native ingredients including produce, herbs, and berries from local farms, shellfish from the surrounding waters, plus fresh game birds and lamb, creates frequently changing menus delightful to the eye as well as the palate. Vineyard residents, visitors, and sailing enthusiasts have created a loyal following for l'étoile's contemporary French flair, enjoying Sunday brunch and evening dining during the balmy summer, and weekends in the quieter winter season.

Soup of Native Mussels with Saffron and Leeks
with Red Pepper and Poppy Seed Breadsticks

*Salad of Softshell Crab,
Avocado, Marinated
Tomatoes, Endive, and Mesclun*
with Lobster and Chardonnay Vinaigrette

*Roasted Veal Sirloin with a Basil and
Parmesan Crust*
Pine Nut and Roasted Garlic Sauce

Fresh Island Raspberries and Blackberries
with Champagne Sabayon Sauce

COLOR PLATE 17

Soup of Native Mussels with Saffron and Leeks
Serves 6

¼ cup shallots, chopped
2 cups dry white wine
2 cloves garlic, crushed
3 cups weak chicken stock
3 pounds mussels, scrubbed, debearded
1 cup heavy cream
½ tablespoon lemon juice
1+ tablespoon saffron threads in ½ cup warm white wine
  (allows control of color and flavor)
Salt and white pepper
6 tablespoons butter
8 tablespoons flour
1 carrot, peeled, julienne
1 medium leek, green removed, cleaned, julienne
1 tablespoon chives, chopped

In a 6- to 8-quart stockpot, heat shallots until they sizzle, add wine, garlic, 1 cup stock, and mussels. Cover and cook over medium-high heat. Remove mussels as they begin to open, place in cold water to stop cooking, remove when cool. Remove ½ the mussels from their shells, reserve remainder.

Bring the cooking liquid to a simmer with 2 cups remaining stock, cream, lemon juice, and saffron liquid, season with salt and pepper. Make a roux of the butter and flour, add to the liquid. Simmer gently for 20 minutes. Skim surface fats, strain through a fine strainer.

To serve, julienne and blanch the carrot and leek, crisscross them in the middle of each soup bowl. Place 3 mussels with shell and 3 without around the julienne, pour broth over the mussels, not covering the vegetables. Sprinkle with chives.

Red Pepper and Poppy Seed Breadsticks
Yield, about 25 breadsticks

½ ounce (1 packet) dry yeast
¼ cup warm water
1 cup milk
4 tablespoons butter
1 teaspoon salt
1 teaspoon sugar
1 red bell pepper, seeded, small diced, lightly sautéed
⅓ cup poppy seeds
1 egg white
3¼ cups flour

Activate the yeast in the warm water with a pinch of sugar. Scald milk, add butter, salt, and sugar, remove from heat, stir until just warm and the butter is melted. Combine the 2 mixtures in a large mixing bowl with the diced pepper and poppy seeds. Beat the egg white with a pinch of salt until stiff, stir into the liquid. Work the flour

into the liquid, knead the dough until firm, adding more flour if sticky. Keep the dough warm allowing to rise until doubled in bulk.

Preheat oven to 400°.

Punch down the dough and cut into breadstick-sized pieces, and roll until long and skinny. Place on a lightly oiled sheet pan and let them rise 15 minutes.

Bake 10 minutes at 400°, then 15 minutes at 300°. Let cool.

Salad of Softshell Crab
Serves 6

6 fresh softshell crabs, cleaned (gills and tails removed)
1 cup flour
3 eggs, beaten
1 cup bread crumbs (plain)
½ cup sesame seeds
½ pound mesclun or mixed salad greens (chicory, radicchio, red and green oak leaf, watercress)
6 ripe plum tomatoes, sliced, marinated in Lobster and Chardonnay Vinaigrette (page 50)
2 bulbs Belgian endive
½ cup peanut oil
1 avocado, peeled, sliced

Dredge crabs (shell sides and legs, not the bottoms) in flour, then eggs, then mixture of bread crumbs and sesame seeds, set aside.

Clean, wash, and spin the greens, arrange on salad plates with tomatoes and endive spears at top of the plates.

Heat peanut oil in a large sauté pan until very hot, place crabs in the pan, shell side up. Cook 4 minutes on medium heat, then turn and cook shell side down until golden brown. Remove crabs to a towel to drain excess oil. Place crabs on a cutting board, shell side down, and quarter with a sharp knife.

Arrange crab on lower half of the greens with avocado slices between the pieces. Drizzle with Lobster and Chardonnay Vinaigrette (page 50).

Lobster and Chardonnay Vinaigrette
Yield, 3 cups

2 medium-size lobster bodies
½ cup olive oil
1 carrot, peeled, thinly sliced
1 stalk celery, thinly sliced
4 shallots, peeled, thinly sliced
2 cloves garlic, crushed
5 ripe plum tomatoes, chopped
1 tablespoon tomato paste
⅓ cup champagne or white wine vinegar
2 cups chardonnay
Salt and pepper
½ teaspoon cayenne pepper, or to taste
1 cup olive oil
¾ cup peanut oil
½ cup champagne or white wine vinegar
2 tablespoons cilantro

Discard shell and eye sack from lobster. Chop the bodies, reserving juices.

Heat ½ cup olive oil in a large sauté pan, add carrot, celery, shallots, and lobster, cover and cook on medium-high for 5 minutes, stirring to assure lobster cooks.

Add the garlic, tomatoes, and tomato paste, cook 10 minutes. Add the vinegar and chardonnay. Simmer covered for 20 minutes and strain into a saucepot, firmly pressing lobster and vegetables to extract maximum juices. Reduce on high heat to 1 cup, season highly with salt, pepper, and cayenne, let cool.

Place liquid in a blender on low speed, adding oil and vinegar alternately until emulsified (thin with water if necessary). Add cilantro, pulse to mix.

❧

Roasted Veal Sirloin with a Basil and Parmesan Crust
Serves 6

4 ounces veal trimmings, cleaned (chicken breast may be substituted for the trimmings)
2 cups basil leaves, packed
½ pound soft butter
2 egg yolks
½ cup Parmesan cheese, grated
1 tablespoon Pommery mustard
1 teaspoon salt
½ teaspoon white pepper
½ cup bread crumbs
½ cup olive oil
6 8-ounce veal top round steaks (or 12-ounce loin chops) trimmed flat and shaped, trimmings reserved

Crust:
Put veal trimmings and basil in a food processor, pulse until meat is pureed. Add butter and egg yolks, pulse until smooth. Add remaining ingredients, pulse until smooth.

Preheat oven to 400°.

Heat olive oil in a large sauté pan and sear the veal steaks on each side until golden brown. Coat 1 side of each steak generously with the crust, smoothing out the top and sprinkling with more bread crumbs. Roast the steaks for 12 minutes until medium rare, browning under a broiler if more color is needed. Serve with Pine Nut and Roasted Garlic Sauce.

Pine Nut and Roasted Garlic Sauce
Yield, about 2½ cups

1 large clove elephant garlic, or 5 cloves regular garlic
1 tablespoon olive oil
1 cup pine nuts
⅓ cup shallots (5), chopped
1 cup dry white wine
2 cups heavy cream
Salt and white pepper

Preheat oven to 350°. Roast garlic in oil in a covered pan until soft to the touch, about 15 minutes. Mash to a puree, adding water if needed.

Roast the pine nuts on a pan in the same oven until golden brown; finely chop ½ the nuts, reserve the balance.

In a heavy-bottomed 2- to 3-quart saucepan, heat the shallots (dry) until they sizzle; add the white wine and chopped pine nuts. Reduce the liquid over medium heat until it barely covers the shallots and nuts. Add the heavy cream and bring to simmer. Use a wire whisk to whip the liquid (off the heat) every 5 minutes. Reduce until sauce coats back of a wooden spoon.

Strain, pressing all juices out of shallots and pine nuts. Season with salt and pepper, flavor with garlic puree to taste. Just before serving add reserved pine nuts to the sauce.

Fresh Island Raspberries and Blackberries with Champagne Sabayon Sauce
Yield, 1½ cups

¼ teaspoon gelatin
2 tablespoons dry champagne
3 egg yolks
⅓ cup sugar
½ cup dry champagne
1 teaspoon lemon juice
Pinch salt
⅓ cup heavy cream, whipped to soft peaks
Fresh raspberries and blackberries, or your favorite variety

Sprinkle gelatin over 2 tablespoons champagne in a small bowl to soften, set aside. In a medium bowl mix the yolks with the sugar and mix over a simmering water bath until warm. Stir in the gelatin mixture, then slowly add the champagne, whisking constantly. Continue to whisk steadily as the mixture cooks. When the mixture is thick and fluffy, whisk rapidly, remove from heat, and place bowl in ice bath to cool. Whisk in the lemon juice and salt. When cool, remove from the ice bath and fold in the whipped cream to give sauce a creamy consistency. Serve over fresh berries. ❧

An Engagement Party

Monticello, next to the Dunhill
Charlotte, North Carolina

Opened in 1929 as the Mayfair Manor apartment hotel, half the original 100 rooms were rented by permanent tenants, including many prominent professionals. Restored in 1987, The Dunhill's lobby and guest rooms blend the elegance of 18th-century European furnishings with original art, hand-sewn draperies, and four-poster beds, creating an unforgettable ambience.

Guests enjoy exceptional dining in the adjacent restaurant, Monticello. "Extraordinary," "poetic," and "inspired" are only a few words that have been used to describe the food at Monticello. Renowned for the brilliant innovation of its ever changing menu, Monticello has also come to represent an explored wine selection that is one of the largest in the Carolinas. A festive atmosphere and celebrated service accompany the unique dining experience.

Corn Soup with Garlic Butter

Ratatouille

Chilled Red and Yellow Tomato Soups
with Peppers, Cucumbers, Onions, and Basil

Grilled Cured Salmon
with Whole Grain Mustard Vinaigrette

COLOR PLATE 18

CORN SOUP WITH GARLIC BUTTER
Serves 6

2 tablespoons unsalted butter
1 medium (6-ounce) onion, diced
4¼ cups water
5 ears fresh corn (1½ pounds), kernels cut from the cob
Salt and black pepper
1 recipe Garlic Butter

Melt the butter in a soup pot and add onion and ¼ cup water, cover and simmer 10 minutes. Add the remaining water and bring to a boil. Add the corn kernels and simmer 5 minutes.

Puree the soup in batches in a blender, allowing blender to run a full 3 minutes for each batch. Press the puree through a coarse sieve, one that will catch the fibers and skins but permit the juice to pass through. Season with ½ teaspoon salt and ⅛ teaspoon pepper, or to taste.

Gently reheat the soup, divide it among heated bowls, garnish each with a dollop of Garlic Butter.

GARLIC BUTTER
Yield, about ⅔ cup

12 cloves garlic (⅓ cup), peeled
Water
Salt
5 tablespoons unsalted butter, softened
¼ teaspoon champagne vinegar
Pinch cayenne
Freshly ground pepper

In a small saucepan, parboil garlic for 1 minute, discard water. Return garlic to the pan. Add 2 cups water, ¼ teaspoon salt, and bring to a boil. Reduce heat and simmer 20 minutes, or until water has almost entirely evaporated and garlic is very soft.

Transfer cloves to a bowl and mash them to a paste with a spatula or spoon. Add the butter, vinegar, cayenne, and season with ⅛ teaspoon salt and a pinch of pepper. Mix well, transfer to a small bowl, cover tightly. Store in a cool place until ready to use, but not longer than 8 hours, as it will become bitter.

RATATOUILLE
Serves 6

Salt and freshly ground black pepper
4 Japanese eggplants (10 ounces), skin on, ¼-inch sliced
¼ cup extra virgin olive oil
¼ cup water
1 large yellow onion (10 ounces), sliced
4 bell peppers (14 ounces), mixed colors, cut into
    ¼-inch strips
2 tablespoons fruity red wine vinegar
4 mixed green and yellow squash (12 ounces), sliced
    crosswise ¼-inch thick
4 medium yellow and red tomatoes (1 pound), peeled,
    seeded, diced, juice discarded
1 tablespoon capers, rinsed, drained
2 tablespoons pitted green or Niçoise olives, chopped
2 tablespoons fresh Italian parsley, chopped
1 tablespoon fresh basil, chopped
2 cloves garlic, minced
Extra virgin olive oil

Preheat oven to 400°.

Salt and pepper the eggplant lightly, toss in a bowl with 3 tablespoons olive oil. Transfer to a baking dish just large enough to contain it and add the water. Cover and bake for about 40 minutes, until soft to the touch.

Meanwhile, sauté the onion in a large saucepot in 3 tablespoons olive oil until it softens and begins to brown lightly. Add the peppers, season with salt and pepper, and cook over high heat, stirring often, until peppers are cooked and onions and pepper are well browned. Add vinegar and cook 1 minute. Transfer the mixture to a bowl, add 2 tablespoons olive oil to the pot and sauté the squash, turning carefully so that both sides are dark brown. Add to the onions and peppers.

Remove eggplant from oven, combine with the vegetables. Discard liquid from the baking dish. Return all vegetables to the saucepot and add tomatoes, stirring only slightly so vegetables do not break up.

Bring to a simmer and cook over medium-high heat for 2 minutes. If the juice seems excessive, pour it into a sauté pan and reduce to thicken, then return it to the vegetables. Remove ratatouille from heat, allow to cool; add capers, olives, parsley, basil, and garlic. Adjust seasonings, if necessary, with more red wine vinegar, salt, and pepper. Before serving, drizzle a little virgin olive oil over each portion.

Chilled Red and Yellow Tomato Soup with Peppers, Cucumbers, Onions, and Basil

Make this beautiful, colorful soup only in summer, when you can choose tomatoes that are very ripe, sweet, and full of juice. Unripe, out-of-season tomatoes make a flavorless, overly acidic soup.

Serves 6

12 very ripe red tomatoes (2½ pounds)
12 very ripe yellow tomatoes (2½ pounds)
⅓ English cucumber (2½ ounces), peeled, ⅛-inch diced
1 small red onion (4 ounces), ⅛-inch diced
½ red bell pepper (2½ ounces), stemmed,
  seeded, ⅛-inch diced
⅛ teaspoon cayenne pepper
2 teaspoons balsamic vinegar
½ teaspoon salt
¼ teaspoon freshly ground pepper
2 tablespoons fresh basil, chopped

Cut the red, then the yellow tomatoes ¼-inch diced, put in separate bowls. Use your hands to squeeze the tomatoes to release as much juice as possible. Keeping the red and yellow tomatoes separate, pass the juice through a stainless steel sieve into nonreactive containers. Push as much of the juice and pulp through as possible. A food mill fitted with a medium blade (smaller than the seeds) may be used. Turn the mill slowly, exerting a downward pressure.

The consistency of the juices will vary, depending on the tomatoes' ripeness. Both soups should be slightly thicker than heavy cream. If too heavy, equalize with a bit of cold water. Similar consistencies are critical.

Mix together the cucumber, onion, and pepper, divide the mixture equally and put ½ in each soup.

To each soup add ½ the measurements of cayenne, balsamic vinegar, salt, pepper, and basil. Place each container of soup in a larger bowl, pack ice around it. Pour water over the ice and refrigerate. Place 6 soup bowls in the refrigerator to chill. It is best to serve the soup at 40°, 1½ to 2 hours after it has been made, when the diced vegetables have released their flavors to the soups.

Use 2 ladles, 1 in each hand, to serve. Scoop equal amounts of the soups (½ cup per ladle) and simultaneously pour them into each half of each chilled bowl. The soups should meet in the middle of the bowl and not blend.

Grilled Cured Salmon
Serves 6

1 2-pound whole fillet of salmon
¼ cup coarse salt
6 3-inch tarragon sprigs
Olive oil

Place fillet of salmon skin-side down, sprinkle with salt, top with sprigs of tarragon. Place the salmon skin-side up in a lightly oiled dish and cover with a damp towel. Refrigerate for 1 day.

Remove the salmon from refrigerator ½ hour before serving. Remove the salt and tarragon, peel off the skin.

Prepare a charcoal fire. Brush salmon lightly with olive oil and place over the hot grill for 2 to 3 minutes on each side, until the salmon feels firm when pressed with a finger. It should remain rare in the center.

Cut the salmon into thin slices and serve with Whole-Grain Mustard Vinaigrette. Fresh spinach is a fine accompaniment.

Whole-Grain Mustard Vinaigrette
Yield, about 1 cup

1 shallot, finely diced
10 to 12 chives, chopped
12 to 15 sprigs chervil, leaves removed
¾ cup light olive oil
Juice of 1 lemon
Salt and pepper
¼ cup whole-grain mustard

Mix the shallot and herbs with the olive oil and lemon juice, season with salt and pepper. Add the whole-grain mustard and whip until all ingredients are blended. ❧

$\mathcal{A}$LOHA!

Sheraton Moana Surfrider
Honolulu, Hawaii

On March 11, 1901, the Moana Hotel—the first resort hotel on Waikiki Beach—opened its doors to the public and a new age. The pride of the budding Hawaiian tourist industry, it was crowded from dawn to midnight with throngs of wide-eyed visitors.

Affectionately called "The First Lady of Waikiki," the hotel holds special significance in the history of the Hawaiian Islands, reflecting an era when gracious hospitality and elegant accommodations provided a special setting for adventurous world-class travelers. Lovingly restored and reopened on March 29, 1989, the Sheraton Moana Surfrider is a cherished treasure, loved not just for its history and its exquisite restoration, but for a tradition of fine dining reflecting Hawaii's marvelous blend of Pacific cultures.

Peking Duck Soup with Wonton

Kahuku Prawns on Green Papaya Salad
with Balsamic Dressing

Medallions of Molokai Venison
and Island Pineapple Onion Relish

Onaga Oriental

Pacific Rim Fresh Fruit Salad
with Lilikoi Sorbet

COLOR PLATE 19

PEKING DUCK SOUP WITH WONTON
Serves 6

1 Peking (or Long Island) duck
1 gallon chicken stock
1 bunch green onions, sliced
1 bunch cilantro, chopped
1 bunch bean sprouts
1 cup ginger root, cracked
1 onion, sliced
1 package wonton

Remove bones from the duck. Setting aside some of the green onion, cilantro, and all of the bean sprouts for garnish, add the duck bones and meat to the cold chicken stock with balance of the vegetables. Bring to a boil and simmer for approximately 2 hours, adding water if necessary.

Slice breast meat into strips, place in soup bowls along with the reserved green onion, cilantro, and bean sprouts. Strain soup through a fine mesh strainer. Heat wonton in the soup, ladle soup into bowls.

KAHUKU PRAWNS ON GREEN PAPAYA SALAD
Serves 6

6 leaves radicchio lettuce
6 leaves oak lettuce
1½ cups green papaya, shredded
Sprig mint leaves
Pinch red bell pepper strips
¾ cup Balsamic Dressing
18 ounces Kahuku prawns (Hawaiian freshwater prawns), fresh or frozen
Olive oil
2 tablespoons peanuts, chopped

Arrange lettuce leaves in a star shape on the plates. Mix papaya, mint, red bell pepper, and Balsamic Dressing, place on top of lettuce leaves.

Sauté prawns in a bit of olive oil until done. Place prawns on top of salad, sprinkle with chopped peanuts.

BALSAMIC DRESSING
Yield, 6 servings

Blend together:
6 tablespoons balsamic vinegar
6 tablespoons vegetable oil
6 tablespoons olive oil
2 tablespoons shallots, chopped
2 tablespoons sun-dried tomato, diced
1 tablespoon Thai basil, chopped
1 teaspoon garlic, chopped
1 tablespoon sugar
½ teaspoon chili peppers, finely chopped
2 tablespoons Thai fish sauce

MEDALLIONS OF MOLOKAI VENISON WITH ISLAND PINEAPPLE ONION RELISH
Serves 6

1 4-pound venison saddle
Dash cracked pepper
¼ cup olive oil
½ cup Maui onion, small diced
½ cup Madeira
1 cup venison stock
9 ounces fresh pineapple, small diced
1 tablespoon butter

Remove venison loin from the bone, clean well. Use bones and scraps to create stock. Cut venison into 12 2½-ounce medallions. Season with cracked pepper, sauté in olive oil until done. Set aside and keep warm.

Discard excess oil from the pan. Sauté onion until brown; deglaze pan with Madeira and add venison stock. Reduce to syruplike consistency. Sauté pineapple in butter and add to onion mixture. Pour pineapple relish into plate, set medallions on top.

Serve with broiled sweet potatoes.

ONAGA ORIENTAL
Serves 6

2 pounds onaga (Hawaiian red snapper) cut into 4-ounce
    fillets, skin on
2 tablespoons vegetable oil
¾ cup shiitake mushrooms, julienne
1 cup snow peas, julienne
¼ cup fish stock
¼ cup fresh ginger root, julienne
2 tablespoons green onion, finely chopped
Cilantro sprigs
2 tablespoons red bell pepper, julienne
Sesame seeds
¼ cup soy sauce
¼ cup sesame oil

*Steam onaga until done (4 minutes). Set aside and
keep warm.*

*Heat a pan with the vegetable oil, add shiitake and
snow peas, sauté briefly. Deglaze with fish stock.*

*Spread sautéed vegetables over serving plates, place
onaga in center. Garnish onaga with ginger, green onion,
cilantro, bell pepper, and a sprinkle of sesame seeds. Pour
soy sauce and hot sesame oil over the garnish.*

PACIFIC RIM FRESH FRUIT SALAD
WITH LILIKOI SORBET
Serves 6

½ to 1 cup each:
    fresh pineapple, sliced
    mango, diced
    papaya, diced
    litchi nuts, whole
    breadfruit, finely sliced
    banana, sliced
3 kiwi, round sliced
6 strawberries, halved
⅓ cup orange juice
2 tablespoons flaked coconut, toasted
Lilikoi (passion fruit) sorbet, or your favorite sorbet
    or sherbet

*Arrange fruits in soup plates, pour orange juice over
the top. Sprinkle with toasted coconut. Place a small scoop
of lilikoi sorbet on top of each.* ❧

A POOLSIDE SPLASH

Stouffer Vinoy Resort
St. Petersburg, Florida

ennsylvania oil man Aymer Vinoy Laughner purchased the site of the Vinoy, overlooking Tampa Bay, in 1923. The Vinoy Park Hotel, a Mediterranean Revival design, was completed one year later, and became a popular resort destination for decades.

The hotel recently enjoyed a $93-million restoration and expansion that added a guest tower and complete recreational facilities, reopening as the 360-room Stouffer Vinoy Resort in the summer of 1992. The Vinoy offers a new 18-hole golf course designed by Ron Garl, a 16-court tennis complex with four different surfaces (home of the Women's Tennis Association), croquet, two heated swimming pools, a 74-slip marina, and a full fitness center with sauna, massage, whirlpool, and steam bath. Four fine restaurants offer a variety of menus to tempt any palate.

Tuna Carpaccio

Roasted Veal
with Tuna Caper Sauce

COLOR PLATE 20

Tuna Carpaccio

For each serving:
2 ounces fresh Ahi (yellowfin) tuna
Ground sea salt
Freshly ground black pepper
⅛ teaspoon black sesame seeds
⅛ teaspoon white sesame seeds
½ teaspoon chives, chopped
1 teaspoon truffle oil
Slice of truffle

Slice tuna paper thin. Cover all of plate with tuna slices, season lightly with salt and pepper. Garnish serving with the sesame seeds, chives, truffle oil, and truffle slice.

Roasted Veal with Tuna Caper Sauce
Serves 6 to 8

6 tablespoons olive oil
1 veal loin
Ground sea salt
Freshly ground black pepper
Tuna Caper Sauce:
12 ounces canned tuna
1 tablespoon capers
Juice of 1 lemon
½ cup plus 2 tablespoons mayonnaise
Italian parsley

Preheat oven to 350°.
Heat 2 tablespoons olive oil in a sauté pan. Season veal loin with salt and pepper and sear it on both sides in the hot pan. Place in the oven and roast for 20 to 30 minutes. The loin should remain pink inside.
Puree tuna, capers, lemon juice, and 4 tablespoons olive oil in a blender. Add mayonnaise, season to taste with salt and pepper (sauce that is too thick may be diluted with the addition of cream or chicken stock).
Once the veal loin is well rested and cold, slice it thin. Place ¼ cup of the tuna sauce on each serving plate, making sure that all of the plate is covered by sauce; arrange 7 thin slices of veal on the sauce. Garnish with parsley leaves and additional capers. ❧

THE WEDDING DAY

Tarrytown House Executive Conference Center
Tarrytown, New York

*E*njoy the splendor of a bygone era at romantic Tarrytown House, a 26-acre estate of two breathtaking 19th-century mansions overlooking the majestic Hudson River. The Greek Revival-styled King House takes its name from one of its previous owners, Thomas King, a wealthy businessman of the late 1800s. The larger, stone chateau-styled Biddle House Mansion was once home to one of America's wealthiest women, Mary Duke Biddle. During the 1920s, her home was a mecca for New York society, who motored up the Hudson in their yachts to attend her lavish parties.

Today, with its broad lawns, winding paths, lush woods, magnificent gardens, impressive dining, and spacious accommodations, Tarrytown House offers the estate experience at its fullest—the perfect site for the most memorable occasions.

Lobster Dijonnaise

Smoked Duck Frisée Mâche
with a Light Walnut Oil and Balsamic Vinegar Dressing

Mandarino Sorbet

Grilled Loin of Veal
with Fresh Spinach, Turned New Potatoes, and
Young Green Beans, with Sweet Red Pepper

Crêpes Amandes Glace

COLOR PLATE 21

LOBSTER DIJONNAISE
Serves 6

3 1¼-pound lobsters
1 cup cooked shrimp, chopped
1 cup Alaskan crabmeat, chopped
¼ cup onion, chopped
¼ cup green pepper, chopped
½ cup red bell pepper, ¼ cup chopped,
  ¼ cup thinly sliced
½ cup mayonnaise
½ cup sour cream
2 tablespoons Dijon mustard
Salt and white pepper
Red leaf lettuce
Fresh chives, chopped
Lemon slices

Cook lobsters in 3 gallons of boiling water approximately 18 minutes. Remove from water and chill in ice water. Split lobsters in half lengthwise from head to tail. Remove meat from claws and tail, rinse shells under cold water. Cut meat from tail into small chunks, reserve meat from claws for garnish. Combine chunked lobster, shrimp, and crab with onion, green pepper, chopped red pepper, mayonnaise, sour cream, mustard, and salt and pepper to taste.

Stuff lobster half-shells with seafood mixture and place on bed of red leaf lettuce. Garnish with sliced red pepper, lobster claw, chives, and lemon.

SMOKED DUCK FRISÉE MÂCHE
6 Servings

10 ounces smoked duck breast
Frisée lettuce (curly endive)
Mâche lettuce
Lo La Rossa lettuce
Orange segments
Walnut-Balsamic Dressing

Slice duck breast thin, 4 slices per person. Arrange lettuces on plate and place duck breast neatly on top, garnish with orange segments. Drizzle with Walnut-Balsamic Dressing at service.

WALNUT-BALSAMIC DRESSING
Yield, 1 cup

⅓ cup balsamic vinegar
⅔ cup walnut oil
Salt and white pepper to taste

Blend ingredients, serve at room temperature.

MANDARINO SORBET
6 Servings

6 mandarin oranges
4 cups mandarin sorbet (frozen puree
  of mandarin oranges)

Cut tops off oranges and hollow out being careful not to scrape through the sides, keep tops. Fill oranges with sorbet, top with small balls of sorbet and replace top. Keep in freezer until needed.

GRILLED LOIN OF VEAL
6 Servings

18 small new potatoes
1½ pounds fresh spinach, steamed
1 pound fresh young green beans (blanched and cold water refreshed)
1 red bell pepper, thinly sliced
2 veal tenderloin

Preheat oven to 350°.

Cut potatoes and steam till tender; steam spinach for 1 to 2 minutes and drain, keep warm; sauté beans lightly with red peppers. Grill veal loin on both sides to sear, then finish in oven till rare (approximately 8 minutes). Slice veal thin and arrange over mounded spinach on plate. Arrange new potatoes, green beans, and peppers. Top with Pink Peppercorn Sauce.

PINK PEPPERCORN SAUCE
Serves 6

1 pound veal bones, oven browned
1 medium carrot
½ garlic bulb
2 celery stalks
1 small tomato
1 bay leaf
Pinch thyme
2 gallons water
½ teaspoon pepper, coarse ground
½ bunch parsley
¼ cup pink peppercorns
Pinch salt

Boil all ingredients except pink peppercorns until reduced to 3 cups. Strain liquid, add pink peppercorns, cook slightly, salt to taste.

CRÊPES AMANDES GLACE
Serves 6

4 egg yolks
1 quart milk
¼ cup butter, melted
1 cup flour
Vanilla ice cream
1½ cups raspberries
Whipped cream
Sliced almonds
Fresh mint leaves, for garnish

Beat egg yolks for 1 minute, blend in milk and butter. Fold in flour (do not beat).

Pour ¼ cup batter in preheated, lightly oiled 8-inch crêpe pan, tilt to distribute evenly. Cook 1½ minutes then flip and cook 1½ minutes more. Place finished crêpes on waxed paper to cool. Place sheets of waxed paper between crêpes, reserve.

Scoop ice cream on crêpes and shape crêpes around ice cream to form a cylinder, freeze. Puree raspberries, reserving some for garnish.

To serve, spread raspberry puree on plate, add crêpe, pipe whipped cream on top of crêpe, sprinkle with sliced almonds. Garnish with fresh mint leaves. ❧

Photography: Mike Wyatt

An Evening for Gourmets
The Greenbrier

Greenbrier Valley Lamb Mixed Grill

COLOR PLATE 14   ON THE FOURTH OF JULY   PAGE 41
The Hay-Adams Hotel

L/R: Chicken and Pepper Salad with Maple Vinaigrette Dressing, Shrimp and Two Cabbage Slaw

COLOR PLATE 15   AN ANTEBELLUM AFTERNOON   PAGE 43
John Rutledge House Inn and King's Courtyard Inn

Plantation Punch

COLOR PLATE 16   DIVING IN THE KEYS   PAGE 45
La Concha, a Holiday Inn Hotel

Lobster-Stuffed Chicken au Grand Marnier

COLOR PLATE 17   AFTER THE REGATTA   PAGE 48
L'etoile, at The Charlotte Inn

A Salad of Softshell Crab with Lobster and Chardonnay Vinaigrette

COLOR PLATE 18   AN ENGAGEMENT PARTY   PAGE 51
Monticello, Next to the Dunhill

Photography: David Franzen

COLOR PLATE 19   ALOHA!   PAGE 54
Sheraton Moana Surfrider

Kahuku Prawns on Green Papaya Salad, with Balsamic Dressing

A POOLSIDE SPLASH
Stouffer Vinoy Resort

L/R: Tuna Carpaccio, Roasted Veal with Tuna Caper Sauce

A UTUMN

$\mathcal{A}$N $\mathcal{A}$MERICAN $\mathcal{T}$HANKSGIVING

The American Club
Kohler, Wisconsin

*T*hanksgiving, the most traditional of American holidays, is beautifully suited to The American Club, established in 1918 as a first home in the new world for European immigrants coming to work for Kohler Co., the growing plumbingware manufacturer.

The original American Club's hallmark holiday feasts continued when the historic structure was converted into a world-class resort hotel in 1981. Today's holiday guests delight in horse-drawn carriage rides, warm themselves in front of a number of roaring fireplaces after cross-country skiing, indulge in the resort's comprehensive spa, and, of course, enjoy the award-winning restaurants, whose innovative regional cooking is evident in this tantalizing interpretation of a Midwestern holiday dinner, perfect for any special occasion.

Great Lakes Chowder

Tricolor Salad with Poached Pears
with Port Wine Vinaigrette
Bresse Bleu Cheese Soufflé

Whole Wheat Walnut Bread
with Dried Cranberry Butter

Hickory-Smoked Wild Tom Turkey
with Sauternes Pan Sauce and
White Wine Grapes and Wild Mushrooms

Pear Pecan Barley

Root Vegetable Julienne with Herb Butter

Bourbon Caramel Apple Gratin

COLOR PLATE 22

GREAT LAKES CHOWDER
Serves 20

4 tablespoons butter
5 large Spanish onions, peeled, diced
4 cloves garlic, chopped
1 bay leaf
3 sprigs fresh thyme, finely chopped
1 gallon clam juice or fish stock
¾ cup roux (equal parts flour and butter,
  cooked 5 minutes)
4 large baking potatoes, peeled, diced
1 quart cream
1 pound smoked chubs, skinned, deboned
1 bunch chives, finely chopped

*Melt butter in a large soup pot and add onions,
garlic, bay leaf, and thyme. Cook slowly, stir.*

Add clam juice and bring to boil, simmer 10 minutes.

*In a small bowl blend the roux with a small amount
of liquid from the soup, incorporate all into the soup,
simmer 20 minutes. Meanwhile, boil the diced potatoes in
a small pot until just tender. Do not overcook. Drain.*

*Stir the cream and potatoes into the soup. Add the
smoked fish, taste for seasoning. (The fish will add salt to
the soup—do not season before adding the fish.)*

Garnish each serving with chopped chives.

TRICOLOR SALAD WITH POACHED PEARS
Serves 6 to 8

3 heads radicchio lettuce
3 heads Belgian endive, washed, leaves removed
1 pound fresh spinach, washed, stemmed

*Separate the radicchio leaves and wash in cold water
leaving them whole, drain well.*

*Combine the greens in a salad bowl. Do not bruise
the leaves with unnecessary handling. Toss with Port Wine
Vinaigrette, allow to sit 10 minutes before serving.*

*Garnish servings with Spiced Poached Pears. Accom-
pany with Bresse Bleu Cheese Soufflé on the side.*

PORT WINE VINAIGRETTE
Yield, about 4 cups

3 cups olive oil
¾ cup fresh herb vinegar
2 lemons, juiced
½ cup port wine
1 clove garlic, chopped
¼ cup shallots, chopped
Fresh thyme and parsley, chopped
Salt, pepper, and sugar to taste

Mix all ingredients together, whip well.

SPICED POACHED PEARS
Yield, variable

3 pears, peeled, left whole
½ cup sugar
4 cups water
1 cup red wine
1 cinnamon stick
6 cloves
1 lemon, sliced

*Reserving pears, combine all ingredients in a saucepot
and simmer. Add the pears, cook until tender, but not
overcooked; test with knife for doneness.*

*The pears may be prepared in advance and refriger-
ated in the liquid. When ready to use, cut into quarters,
core, slice into ⅛-inch slices.*

BRESSE BLEU CHEESE SOUFFLÉ
Serves 6 to 8

4 tablespoons butter
4 tablespoons flour
1½ cups milk
6 egg yolks
1 pound Bresse bleu cheese, medium grated
½ teaspoon ground black pepper
6 egg whites

*Melt the butter in a saucepot and add the flour, stir
into a roux and cook for 5 minutes. Add the milk and
whisk until smooth. Remove from heat and allow to cool.*

*Stir in the egg yolks 2 at a time, then the grated cheese
and pepper.*

Preheat oven to 400°.

*Whip egg whites until they form stiff peaks. Fold ⅓ of
the whites into the soufflé to lighten it, then fold in the
balance. Fill a greased soufflé dish ¾ full, bake in a
water bath for 15 to 20 minutes or until a straw inserted
can be removed without sticking. Serve immediately.*

WHOLE WHEAT WALNUT BREAD
Yield, 3 loaves

1 package dry yeast
2½ cups warm water (105° - 115°)
1 tablespoon honey
1 tablespoon brown sugar
½ cup nonfat dry milk
2 tablespoons butter, softened
2 teaspoons salt
1 cup bread flour
4½ cups whole wheat flour
2½ cups walnut pieces
Egg wash (1 egg mixed with 2 tablespoons milk)

*Put yeast in a large bowl and add warm water, blend
in honey and brown sugar. Stir in dry milk, butter, and
salt. Stir in bread flour.* (Continued, page 66.)

Add whole wheat flour ½ cup at a time until batter is thick and difficult to stir. Let batter rest 3 to 4 minutes while large particles absorb moisture—the dough will be sticky. Turn the ball of dough onto a floured work surface and knead for 5 minutes.

Return the dough to a greased bowl and cover with plastic wrap and leave at room temperature until doubled in bulk, from 1 to 1¼ hours. Place dough on work surface and flatten it. Pour ½ the nuts in the center and fold in. Repeat with the balance of the nuts.

Divide dough into 2 or 3 equal parts and shape into a smooth ball or loaf. Place on a baking sheet. Cover with waxed paper and leave at room temperature for about 50 minutes.

Preheat oven to 375°.

Brush loaves with egg wash. Make 3 to 4 shallow cuts with a razor blade. Bake in middle of oven for 40 to 50 minutes or until darkly browned. Cool on wire rack.

DRIED CRANBERRY BUTTER
Yield, 1 pound

½ cup dried cranberries
2 cups cranberry juice
Zest of 1 orange
3 tablespoons sugar
1 pound butter, softened

Slowly simmer the cranberries in the juice with the orange zest and sugar until they absorb the liquid. Set aside to cool.

Use a food processor to chop the cranberries fine. Add the butter and blend until evenly mixed, scraping down the sides of the processor while mixing.

Serve the butter in a crock or pipe into stars.

HICKORY-SMOKED WILD TOM TURKEY
Serves 5

1 10-pound tom turkey, giblets removed, cavity well rinsed

Brine:
2 gallons water
1¾ cups salt
1 pound sugar
6 teaspoons whole cloves
2 tablespoons black pepper, ground
1 pound brown sugar
3 tablespoons Cajun seasoning
1 teaspoon dry thyme
2 tablespoons garlic, chopped

Combine the brine ingredients and stir until salt and sugar are dissolved. Submerge the turkey in the brine and refrigerate for 2 days, turning the turkey and stirring the brine to achieve uniform seasoning.

For smoking:
2 pounds hickory chips

Soak hickory chips in water overnight. Start charcoal in an outdoor grill, heating coals to the point of being white with ash. Remove hickory chips from water, shake off excess water. Put the wood chips on the charcoal and allow them to begin producing smoke.

Remove turkey from the brine, place on grill high enough above the fire to avoid browning. Cover grill, adjust air vents to control the fire. Should the chips begin to burn, spray with a water mist from a spray bottle.

Smoke the turkey for about 2 hours, finish cooking by pan-roasting in a 350° oven until turkey reaches an internal temperature of 130° to 140°.

SAUTERNES PAN SAUCE
Yield, about 4 cups

2 large onions, finely sliced
2 cloves garlic, peeled, chopped
2 sprigs fresh thyme, stemmed, chopped
2 cups Sauternes
1 quart chicken stock or bouillon
Cornstarch and water to thicken
Salt and pepper

Remove turkey from roasting pan, skim excess fat. Sauté the onions, garlic, and thyme in the roasting pan until well caramelized, but not burnt.

Deglaze pan with wine and reduce by ½. Add chicken stock and simmer. Thicken lightly with combination of cornstarch and water. Season with salt and pepper.

WHITE WINE GRAPES AND WILD MUSHROOMS
Serves 4

4 tablespoons butter
6 shallots, peeled, chopped
1½ pounds assorted wild mushrooms (oyster, shiitake, chanterelle, morel, button) as available
1 pound seedless white grapes, stemmed, halved
Salt and pepper

Melt the butter in a large sauté pan. Sauté shallots lightly and add mushrooms and grapes—do not overcook. Season to taste. Serve with the turkey.

PEAR PECAN BARLEY
page 112

ROOT VEGETABLE JULIENNE
page 112

HERBED BUTTER
page 112

BOURBON CARAMEL APPLE GRATIN
page 113

LUNCH FOR AN AUTUMN FOLIAGE TOUR

The Equinox Hotel, Resort & Spa
Manchester Village, Vermont

A blend of 223 years of intriguing history, 6 architectural styles, 17 buildings, and a roster of 7 different names, the Equinox is a study in Americana. Shuttered for a decade, the hotel reopened in 1985 after years of historical studies lead to its renovation. Inside and out, every detail was restored to its original beauty, features now augmented by a spa and a myriad of recreational opportunities.

Located on Historic Route 7 in the lush countryside of south-central Vermont, the Equinox has been host to generations of travelers. Browse in The Equinox Shops, or visit nearby historic landmarks and theaters. Should your travels bring you to New England to view the world-famous autumn foliage, you will simply find no more welcome accommodations than The Equinox.

Gingered Apple and Butternut Bisque
with Pumpernickel Sippets

Salad of Grilled Fall Radicchio
with Pickled Harvest Vegetables

Roasted Breast of Vermont Pheasant
with Autumn Cranberries and Persimmons
and Maple Potato Cakes

Chestnut Corn Bread

Pumpkin Cheesecake with Cider Sauce

COLOR PLATE 23

GINGERED APPLE AND BUTTERNUT BISQUE WITH PUMPERNICKEL SIPPETS

Serves 6

¼ pound butter
2 onions, diced
½ leek, cleaned, diced
2 carrots, diced
6 shallots, diced
5 large butternut squash, skinned, diced
6 McIntosh apples, cored, skinned, diced
2 teaspoons fresh ginger, diced
1 pinch thyme
3 bay leaves
1 teaspoon vanilla extract
1 cup Vermont maple syrup
½ teaspoon cinnamon
Pinch nutmeg
2 cups white wine
2 quarts chicken stock
Salt and pepper

Garnish:
Lightly sweetened whipped cream
Pumpernickel sippets (triangular croutons)

Melt butter in a roasting pan and cook the onions, leeks, carrots, and shallots until tender.

Preheat oven to 325°.

Add to the pan the squash, apples, ginger, thyme, bay leaves, vanilla, maple syrup, cinnamon, and nutmeg, cook in the oven until squash is tender. Deglaze the pan with the white wine.

Transfer ingredients from the roasting pan to a soup pot. Add the chicken stock and simmer until the squash is completely cooked. Remove bay leaves.

Use a food processor to puree the soup until it is smooth and creamy. Reheat to serve, adjusting seasoning with salt and pepper. Serve with slightly sweetened whipped cream and pumpernickel sippets.

❧

ROASTED BREAST OF VERMONT PHEASANT

Serves 6

3 3-pound pheasants, breasts removed and split,
   carcasses reserved

Marinade:
1 tablespoon each of juniper berries, mustard seeds, and
   black peppercorns
1 clove garlic, roasted
1 quart apple cider
¼ cup dried cranberries, finely chopped
6 sprigs fresh rosemary
6 sprigs fresh thyme
¼ cup each of balsamic vinegar and maple syrup
4 bay leaves
1 tablespoon salt

Blend ingredients. Marinate pheasant breasts for 4 to 6 hours, or overnight. Prepare stock.

Pheasant stock:
Reserved pheasant carcasses
1 large onion, chopped
2 carrots, chopped
1 leek, rinsed, chopped
4 shallots, peeled
2 bay leaves
A few sprigs of fresh parsley and thyme
1 teaspoon black pepper
1 cup white wine

Rinse carcasses thoroughly. Place in a small stockpot, cover with cold water (at least 2 quarts). Add balance of ingredients, simmer gently until liquid is reduced to 1 quart, strain. Reserve for Cranberry-Persimmon Sauce.

Preheat oven to 350°.

Place an iron skillet on the stove top, heat just enough oil to sear breasts. When oil is hot, remove breasts from marinade, tapping to remove excess liquid. Sear the breasts on both sides, pour off excess oil.

Add some of the marinade to the skillet to avoid oven-scorching. Roast the pheasant for 10 minutes, using the marinade to baste while roasting.

Place a portion of the Cranberry-Persimmon Sauce on each serving plate, top each with ½ pheasant breast, garnish with quartered persimmons and fresh herbs. Accompany with Maple Potato Cakes.

CRANBERRY-PERSIMMON SAUCE

Yield, about 3 cups

3 tablespoons hazelnut oil
6 shallots, diced
2 large persimmons, diced
1 cup fresh cranberries
¼ cup tomato paste
¼ cup red wine vinegar
1 cup port wine
1 quart pheasant stock
Arrowroot and port wine, as needed, for thickening

Heat oil in sauté pan, add shallots, sauté gently. Add persimmons and cranberries, sauté lightly. Add tomato paste, cook briefly.

Deglaze pan with vinegar, add the port, reduce by ½; add the pheasant stock and reduce by ⅓. When reduced, puree sauce in a food processor.

At service time, reheat sauce and adjust thickness, if needed, with a paste of arrowroot and port wine. Season to taste with salt and pepper.

MAPLE POTATO CAKES
Yield, 6 cakes

2 Yukon Gold potatoes
2 sweet potatoes
½ onion, finely grated
2 tablespoons potato starch
½ teaspoon maple syrup
1 egg yolk
Salt and white pepper to taste
Oil, for cooking

Peel and shred the potatoes, squeezing out excess moisture. Mix the onions, potato starch, maple syrup, egg yolk, and salt and pepper with the potatoes.

Form the shredded potatoes into silver-dollar-sized pancakes and sauté slowly in hot oil until lightly browned. Turn and brown the second side. Drain briefly, serve.

❧

SALAD OF GRILLED FALL RADICCHIO
Serves 6

¼ cup equal parts coriander seeds, and red, green, and
  black peppercorns
1 cup virgin olive oil
¼ cup cider vinegar
3 small, firm heads radicchio
Kosher salt

Use a spice grinder to finely chop the coriander and peppercorns, reserve. Combine the olive oil and vinegar in a bowl. Split radicchio into quarters and dip into the oil/vinegar mixture, season with the ground spices and salt.

Sear radicchio over hot coals (it needs only to be grilled a few seconds, long enough to pick up a grilled flavor).

Arrange grilled radicchio on salad plates, accompany with Pickled Harvest Vegetables. At serving time, sprinkle some of the vegetable marinade over the radicchio.

PICKLED HARVEST VEGETABLES
Yield, variable

For marinade, blend:
2 cups olive oil
1 cup cider vinegar
1 bunch fresh thyme
8 shallots, peeled, finely chopped
¼ cup honey
1 teaspoon salt
1 tablespoon white peppercorns, cracked

Select traditional, late season root vegetables such as beets, turnips, parsnips, boiling onions, and sweet bliss potatoes. Mushrooms, herbs, and tomatoes can also be used. Clean vegetables and cut into serving sizes. Marinate the vegetables overnight.

❧

CHESTNUT CORN BREAD
Yield, 1 9 x 13-inch pan

1 cup vegetable oil
¾ cup eggs
1½ cups sugar
1½ cups each of pastry flour and bread flour
1 cup cornmeal
4 tablespoons baking powder
1½ teaspoons salt
3 cups milk
1 cup roasted chestnuts
¼ cup chives, minced

Preheat oven to 350°. Blend together vegetable oil and eggs. Alternately add the dry ingredients with the milk. Blend thoroughly, but do not overmix. Add chestnuts and chives, pour into ungreased 9 x 13 x 2-inch pan, bake 30 minutes, until done.

To roast chestnuts:
Preheat oven to 300°.
Split chestnuts' shells with a sharp knife. Place chestnuts on a shallow roasting pan, roast for 30 minutes. Remove from oven, cool, remove nutmeats.

❧

PUMPKIN CHEESECAKE
Yield, 1 9-inch cheesecake

Shell:
2½ cups gingersnap cookie crumbs
Melted butter

Moisten cookie crumbs with melted butter, press into the bottom of a 9-inch springform pan. Set aside.

Cheesecake:
24 ounces cream cheese
¾ cup sugar
4 eggs
12 ounces prepared pumpkin (not pie mix)
1 teaspoon vanilla extract
1½ cups heavy cream

Preheat oven to 325°.
In a large mixing bowl, beat together the cream cheese and sugar until smooth. Add eggs 1 at a time, blending well after each addition. Add pumpkin and vanilla, mix well. Finish blending completely while adding cream. Fill gingersnap shell with the batter, bake in a water bath for 1½ hours.
Serve with Cider Sauce and whipped cream.

CIDER SAUCE
Yield, 1 cup

1 quart apple cider

Simmer apple cider until reduced to 1 cup. The sauce will have a jelly-like consistency. Cool before serving. ❧

AFTER THE THEATER

The Heathman Hotel
Portland, Oregon

*B*uilt in 1927 on Broadway—Portland's "Great White Way"—The Heathman's proximity to the city's cultural center has made it a traditional meeting spot before and after performances. The Heathman enthusiastically supports the Oregon Shakespeare Festival, the Oregon Symphony, Portland Arts and Lectures, Portland Opera, and other cultural organizations. Connected to the Performing Arts Center, the hotel has a door opening directly into the first balcony of the historic Schnitzer Concert Hall.

Patrons enjoy The Heathman Restaurant before performances and the cozy Mezzanine Library or Bar for after-theater nightcaps. Chef Greg Higgins creates diverse menus to suit the palates of culture enthusiasts. Following is his suggestion for a delightful after-theater dinner.

Spiced Winter Squash Bisque

Salad of Winter Greens
in Raspberry Vinaigrette

Medallions of Veal
with Forest Mushrooms,
Whole-Grained Mustard, and Späetzle

Walnut Caramel Tart

COLOR PLATE 24

SPICED WINTER SQUASH BISQUE
Serves 8

2 large yellow onions, peeled, coarsely chopped
2 tablespoons garlic, chopped
2 tablespoons curry powder
3 tablespoons olive oil
3 pounds winter squash (acorn, butternut, delicata, or other), peeled, deseeded
2 quarts chicken stock
Salt and pepper
½ cup hazelnuts or walnuts, toasted, chopped

In a large saucepan over medium heat, sauté the onions, garlic, and curry with the olive oil. Cut the squash into 1-inch chunks. When the onions are tender (5 to 7 minutes) add the squash and chicken stock. Bring to a simmer and season with salt and pepper to taste. Simmer for 1 to 1½ hours until the squash is very tender.

Puree in small batches in a blender or food processor and serve garnished with the toasted nuts.

SALAD OF WINTER GREENS IN RASPBERRY VINAIGRETTE
Yield, variable

For each guest, wash and prepare 1 to 2 cups of crisp winter salad greens such as endive, spinach, oakleaf lettuce, plus chanterelle mushrooms, or your favorite selection. Toss gently with the Raspberry Vinaigrette, serve.

RASPBERRY VINAIGRETTE
Yield, 3 cups

¼ cup Dijon mustard
2 tablespoons black pepper
¼ cup shallots, finely chopped
2 cups canola or other light salad oil
1 cup raspberry vinegar
Salt and pepper

Combine mustard, black pepper, and shallots in a mixing bowl or food processor. Gradually whisk in oil ½ cup at a time until the mixture is fully blended and emulsified. Gradually whisk in the raspberry vinegar and adjust seasoning to taste with salt and pepper.

RASPBERRY VINEGAR
Yield, 2 cups

1 pint fresh raspberries
2 cups white wine or champagne vinegar

Marinate raspberries at room temperature in the vinegar for at least two weeks. Strain.

MEDALLIONS OF VEAL WITH FOREST MUSHROOMS AND WHOLE-GRAIN MUSTARD
Serves 8

3 pounds veal loin mignons (6- to 8-ounce medallions)
Salt and pepper
Flour
2 to 3 tablespoons oil
3 pounds mixed forest mushrooms, cleaned, sliced
2 cups shallots, chopped
½ cup whole-grain mustard
1 bottle pinot blanc or pinot gris
1 quart veal or chicken stock
2 cups heavy cream

Lightly pound the veal medallions until they are an even thickness, about ½ inch. Season with salt and pepper and lightly dredge in flour, shake off excess. In a large pan on medium-high heat, sear veal in hot oil about 1 minute on each side. Place medallions in a baking pan and set aside.

Use the same pan to sauté mushrooms and shallots over medium heat. When mushrooms are nearly done (3 to 5 minutes) remove them from the pan and add the mustard, wine, and stock. Reduce over medium/medium-high heat until it begins to thicken and will coat a spoon. Add the heavy cream and mushrooms, continue to reduce.

Preheat oven to 400°.

Place the pan with the medallions in the preheated oven, roast to desired doneness (5 to 7 minutes for medium-rare to medium). Serve the medallions over the sauce on serving plates, accompanied by buttered Späetzle.

SPÄETZLE
Serves 8

4½ cups flour
4 eggs
3 tablespoons heavy cream
Salt, pepper, and nutmeg, to taste
Butter

Combine the first 4 ingredients, mix until smooth.

Cook by forcing through a very coarse colander into boiling salted water. Cook until firm, drain.

Lightly sauté in butter, serve.

WALNUT CARAMEL TART
Yield, 10 servings

Crust:

1½ cups all-purpose flour

2 tablespoons sugar

Pinch salt

8 tablespoons unsalted butter

1 egg yolk

1 tablespoon ice water

Combine flour, sugar, and salt in a mixing bowl; cut in butter until the mixture resembles coarse crumbs. Add egg yolk and water and mix with fork until dough begins to mass together. Gather into a ball, cover with plastic wrap, refrigerate 30 minutes.

Roll out pastry on a lightly floured surface; use it to line a 9-inch tart pan. Chill ½ hour.

Preheat oven to 400°.

Cover tart shell with waxed or parchment paper and weight the surface with dried beans (or rice). Bake 15 minutes. Remove the paper and beans. Lightly prick bottom of pastry shell with a fork, continue baking until the shell is golden brown. Remove from oven and cool.

Filling:

1⅔ cups sugar

¾ cup water

½ cup lemon juice

¾ cup whipped cream

½ teaspoon orange rind, grated

9 tablespoons butter, cut in pieces

1⅓ cups walnuts, lightly roasted, chopped

Combine sugar, water, and lemon juice in a saucepan. Bring to a boil and cook without stirring until caramelized. Add cream, stir until lumps dissolve. Add orange rind and butter to caramel, whisk until smooth. Stir in walnuts and pour into prepared tart shell. Chill until firm.

Glaze:

2 ounces bittersweet chocolate

1⅓ tablespoons water

2 tablespoons butter

10 walnut halves, for decoration

Melt chocolate in water in a bowl set over hot water. Remove from heat and stir in the butter until blended. Pour over the tart and spread to cover the tart filling. Let the glaze set; score tart into 10 portions. Decorate each serving with a walnut half. ❧

$\mathcal{A}$ $\mathcal{D}$AY OF $\mathcal{H}$ORSEBACK $\mathcal{R}$IDING

The Homestead
Hot Springs, Virginia

$\mathcal{M}$any Homestead traditions spring from the resort's beautiful setting in the Allegheny Mountains of Virginia. Over 100 miles of scenic riding trails that crisscross the 15,000 lushly wooded acres make horseback riding a favorite Homestead pastime. Lessons for beginners and a show ring for more experienced equestrians make The Homestead the perfect place for a riding holiday. Those who would rather not get in the saddle can experience the charm of The Homestead's early days with a ride in a horsedrawn carriage. After a day's ride in the mountains, guests can dine in the casual fireside atmosphere of Sam Snead's Tavern or in the elegant Dining Room. The following recipes are Homestead specialties that Chef Albert has chosen as a perfect evening complement to an afternoon on the trails.

French Venison Stew

Späetzle

Roast Double Breast of Turkey
with Ham, Apricot, and Pecan Stuffing

Homestead Corn Pudding

Acorn Squash with Honey

Sweet Potatoes Duchesse

Double Applesauce Cake

COLOR PLATE 25

French Venison Stew
Serves 6 to 8

3 pounds boneless venison shoulder, chuck, or leg

Marinade:
1 medium onion, coarsely chopped
1 celery stalk (leaves removed), coarsely chopped
½ medium carrot, coarsely chopped
1 clove garlic, peeled
6 juniper berries
½ bay leaf
1 small clove
Pinch thyme
3 tablespoons red wine vinegar
2 cups dry red wine (or as needed to completely
  cover venison)

Trim venison, cut into 1½-inch cubes. Place venison and all other ingredients in a nonreactive bowl, mix well, cover bowl with plastic wrap, marinate refrigerated 2 to 6 days.

Strain meat and vegetables, reserve marinade. Separate and reserve vegetables, drain venison on absorbent toweling.

For braising:
1 4- to 5-ounce bacon slab
2 tablespoons peanut oil
Salt and black pepper, freshly ground
Reserved vegetables
2 tablespoons flour
1 tablespoon tomato paste
Strained marinade
1½ cups demi-glace

Trim rind from bacon, cut into 1½ inch lardons (cubes). In a Dutch oven over medium heat, sauté lardons, stirring, until crisp; remove to absorbent towels. Add peanut oil to the bacon fat, increase heat to high; season venison with salt and pepper, sauté in batches until all is browned.

Return venison to the pot, add reserved vegetables, sprinkle with flour, sauté until flour browns. Stir in tomato paste, mix well, sauté 1 minute. Add marinade liquid and deglaze the pot, scraping browned bits from bottom, simmer about 5 minutes until sauce is smooth. Add demi-glace, return sauce to simmer, cover, maintain at gentle simmer for 1 to 1½ hours, or until venison is tender.

Sautéed mushrooms:
12 large fresh mushrooms, cleaned, halved
1½ teaspoons clarified butter
Salt and black pepper, freshly ground
½ lemon, juiced

Over medium heat, sauté mushrooms with butter for 3 minutes, season with salt, pepper, and lemon juice.

Sautéed onions:
12 small white onions, whole, or 48 pearl onions
1½ teaspoons clarified butter
½ teaspoon sugar

Bring lightly salted water to boil in a small pan, add onions, boil 10 minutes (pearl onions need to be boiled only 2 minutes). Rinse onions with cold water, drain, and peel. Add butter to a sauté pan over medium low heat, add sugar and onions, sauté until lightly browned and glazed, 4 to 5 minutes. Drain oil, add the onions to the mushrooms.

Croutons:
2 slices heavy bread
1 tablespoon clarified butter

Cut the bread into crouton slices 2 inches long and ½-inch wide. Sauté in hot butter over medium heat until golden brown. Drain on absorbent towels, reserve.

To serve:
Sautéed mushrooms and onions
Reserved lardons
Croutons
1 teaspoon fresh parsley, chopped

When venison is tender, remove with a slotted spoon to a large saucepan. Pour sauce through a sieve into a bowl, discard vegetables. (For a heartier "Hunter Stew", you may choose to leave the vegetables in the stew.) Return sauce to Dutch oven and skim the fat. When degreased, adjust seasonings if necessary, pour sauce over the venison; set over medium-low heat, add mushrooms and onions, bring to a gentle simmer to heat through.

Present the stew in a serving dish or on warmed dinner plates. Sprinkle with reserved lardons, croutons, and parsley.

❦

Späetzle
Serves 6

1 cup milk, lukewarm
3 cups all-purpose flour
¼ teaspoon salt
⅛ teaspoon white pepper, freshly ground
¼ teaspoon nutmeg, freshly ground
5 eggs
2 tablespoons butter

Warm milk over low heat. In a mixing bowl, stir together the flour, salt, pepper, and nutmeg. Pour the milk into a small bowl, whisk in the eggs 1 at a time. Make a well in the flour, pour in the liquid, stir thoroughly until smooth, then stir with continuous strokes until bubbles begin to form on the surface.

Set a large saucepan of water to a steady boil, salt lightly. Force the dough through a colander or späetzle maker in batches. When the späetzle float, skim them from the water, set in a sieve, rinse with cold water 5 seconds, drain thoroughly. Reserve on a large, flat pan.

At serving time, add butter to a sauté pan over medium heat. Sauté späetzle, stirring, until lightly browned.

Roast Double Breast of Turkey
Serves 8 to 10

1 8- to 12-pound fresh turkey, boned
Salt and white pepper, freshly ground
½ teaspoon fresh rosemary
2 tablespoons peanut oil
½ medium carrot, coarsely chopped
1 stalk celery, coarsely chopped
1 medium onion, quartered
1 cup dry white wine

Sauce:
1½ tablespoons Dijon mustard
1½ cups heavy cream
2 tablespoons glace de viande

Lay breast meat on work surface and spread skin from thighs and legs, keeping skin intact. With knife parallel to work surface, slice breast in half lengthwise. Remove top layer of meat, set on thigh and leg skin. Spread Ham, Apricot, and Pecan Stuffing on the center of the breast and form a roll by folding the skin over the stuffing from both sides. Tie at 2-inch intervals, season with salt and pepper, rub with rosemary.

Preheat oven to 400°.

Put peanut oil in roasting pan, lay turkey roll in the pan, breast meat down, set pan in oven. Allow to roast 15 minutes after it begins sizzling. Reduce heat to 325°, cook for 45 minutes.

Turn the turkey over, strew with carrot, celery, and onion, add wine. Roast 30 additional minutes, turn again, cook for 15 minutes more. Remove from oven, set turkey on platter, cover loosely with foil, allow to rest 15 minutes.

Transfer juices and vegetables to a saucepan over medium heat. Add mustard, cream, and glace de viande; bring to boil, reduce by ½ to creamy consistency, 10 to 15 minutes. Strain into another saucepan, adjust seasonings, keep warm.

Add any juices from platter to the sauce. Cut strings on turkey, slice ¼-inch thick. To serve, spoon sauce onto serving plates or a platter, top with slices of turkey.

Ham, Apricot, and Pecan Stuffing
Serves 8 to 10

1 tablespoon peanut oil
8 ounces Virginia ham, ¼-inch diced
2 stalks celery, finely diced
½ medium onion, finely diced
1 pound veal trimmings (shoulder or chuck)
  twice ground
¼ cup fresh parsley, chopped
½ cup dried apricots, finely sliced
¾ cup pecans
⅓ cup raisins
½ cup fine white bread crumbs
1 cup half-and-half
Salt and white pepper, freshly ground

In a sauté pan over medium heat, heat peanut oil; sauté ham, celery, and onion for 2 minutes, stirring occasionally. Set aside to cool.

Mix together veal, parsley, apricots, pecans, raisins, bread crumbs, half-and-half, and ham mixture. Season with salt and pepper to taste. Chill completely before use.

Homestead Corn Pudding
Serves 10

3½ cups milk
1 cup yellow cornmeal
3 tablespoons sugar
⅓ teaspoon salt
3 large eggs
¼ teaspoon vanilla extract
1 teaspoon baking powder
1 8-ounce can whole kernel corn, including liquid
4 tablespoons butter, at room temperature

Preheat oven to 300°.

Heat milk to boiling point over medium heat; while stirring constantly with a whisk, mix in cornmeal, sugar, and salt; reduce heat to simmer, cook, stirring, for 5 minutes; remove from heat.

Beat eggs well and add them to the saucepan along with the vanilla, baking powder, corn and liquid, and 2 tablespoons butter. Mix thoroughly, pour into a baking dish, dot with remaining butter, and bake until lightly browned, about 20 minutes. Serve piping hot. ❧

Acorn Squash with Honey
page 113

Sweet Potatoes Duchesse
page 114

Double Applesauce Cake
page 114

TASTE OF THE SOUTH
The Jefferson, a Grand Heritage Hotel
Richmond, Virginia

Built by tobacco tycoon Major Louis Ginter, The Jefferson opened on October 31, 1895, and was promptly hailed as one of the finest hotels in the country. Damaged by fire in 1901, The Jefferson was enlarged and renovated between 1905 and 1907, and offered novel features including fish and alligator ponds in The Palm Court, a lower lobby with faux marble columns, stained glass skylights, and a place of prominence for the noted Edward V. Valentine sculpture of Thomas Jefferson.

The hotel's signature restaurant, Lemaire, is named for Thomas Jefferson's White House maître d'hôtel, credited with introducing America to the fine art of cooking with wine. Lemaire's critically acclaimed menu features fine Southern cooking—fresh ingredients and a refined blending of traditional textures and flavors.

A Salad of Virginia Greens
with Raspberry Vinaigrette

Crab and Corn Chowder

Oysters Jefferson

Loin of Lamb in Pastry

Pear Tart

COLOR PLATE 26

A SALAD OF VIRGINIA GREENS
Serves 6

1 pound greens, including any 5 of the following:
  red oak lettuce, curly endive, sorrel, kale, chicory,
  nasturtium, mâche, dandelion
3 tomatoes, cut into eighths
1 cucumber, halved lengthwise, sliced
3 radishes, fine julienne

Wash greens, drain thoroughly, and place on serving plates. Garnish perimeter of each plate with 4 tomato and 4 cucumber slices, sprinkle with radish julienne. Drizzle with Raspberry Vinaigrette.

RASPBERRY VINAIGRETTE
Yield, 4½ cups

1 pint fresh raspberries, pureed
¾ cup raspberry or red wine vinegar
1½ teaspoons basil, chopped
½ teaspoon each of chopped oregano, thyme, and shallot
¼ teaspoon garlic, finely chopped
2 cups olive or high-grade vegetable oil
2 tablespoons sugar
Salt and pepper

Whisk together raspberries, vinegar, herbs, shallots, and garlic in medium mixing bowl, slowly adding oil. Adjust flavor with sugar, season with salt and pepper to taste.

CRAB AND CORN CHOWDER
Serves 6 to 8

1 stick butter
1 medium white onion, ¼-inch dice
1½ cups cut corn
1 large Idaho potato, peeled, ½-inch dice
¼ cup all-purpose flour
1 quart chicken stock
1 pint heavy cream
2 tablespoons dry sherry
1 tablespoon cornstarch
½ pound fresh crabmeat
Salt and pepper

Melt the butter in a heavy 4-quart pot over medium heat; add onion and cook 2 minutes, stirring often. Add corn and potatoes, cook 2 minutes, taking care not to brown. While cooking, add the flour and stir until the liquid is absorbed and a paste is formed, about 1 minute. Add chicken stock and whisk briskly to remove lumps, bring to a boil, stirring often. Boil 2 minutes. Add the cream and return to a boil for 2 minutes.

In a small bowl combine sherry and cornstarch and add to the pot, stirring often. Return to boil, reduce heat to simmer. Add crabmeat, cook 5 minutes. Season to taste with salt and pepper.

OYSTERS JEFFERSON
Serves 6

Pancakes:
½ cup all-purpose flour, sifted
¼ cup yellow cornmeal
4 tablespoons cold water
1 cup milk
2 large eggs
4 tablespoons unsalted butter, melted

Place flour and cornmeal in a mixing bowl.

In another bowl blend water, milk, and eggs. Slowly add to the dry ingredients. Mix in butter.

Heat a nonstick pan to medium high. Brush the pan with oil and cook pancakes. The yield should be 24 half-dollar size pancakes.

Oyster garni:
2 quarts water
1¼ cups white wine
3 tablespoons lemon juice
24 medium oysters, shucked
1½ cups hollandaise sauce
1 bunch parsley
8 ounces Smithfield ham, julienne

In a saucepot bring to boil the water, wine, and lemon juice. Add oysters and poach for 2 minutes.

On each serving plate, arrange 4 pancakes at the 3, 6, 9 and 12 o'clock positions. Place 1 oyster on each cake, top with hollandaise. Place 4 sprigs of parsley in the center of each plate, garnish the space between each oyster/pancake with a pinch of ham julienne.

LOIN OF LAMB IN PASTRY
Serves 6

1 pound collard or mustard greens
2 ham hocks
Water to cover
3 lamb loins (from center of rack), bones and
　trimmings reserved for stock
4 tablespoons cooking oil
1 sheet puff pastry
Flour
2 eggs, beaten, for egg wash
Lamb Glaze

Place greens in a pot with the ham hocks, add water to cover. Bring to a boil, simmer for 1 hour, or until greens are tender. Remove ham hocks, drain, reserve greens.

Sear lamb loins in a hot pan with the cooking oil, remove from heat.

Preheat oven to 400°.

Place sheet of puff pastry on work surface, cover with flour, and roll out the dough until it is 1½ times its original size. Cut dough into 3 equal parts. Place a thin layer of greens over the dough, top with a lamb loin, wrapping the dough around the loin. Place the loin on a sheet pan, and egg wash. Bake for 18 minutes or until golden brown.

To serve, pour a portion of the Lamb Glaze on each serving plate. Slice the loins thin and place portions on the glaze. (Each loin yields 2 portions.)

LAMB GLAZE
Yield, 2½ cups

2 gallons lamb stock
½ cup bourbon
4 tablespoons cornstarch, if needed
4 tablespoons water, if needed

Make a stock (at least 2 gallons) from reserved rack bones and trimmings. Reduce the stock to about 2½ cups of glaze. Flame the bourbon to remove the alcohol, and add it to the glaze. If desired, the sauce may be thickened with a mixture of cornstarch and water.

PEAR TART
Serves 6

Pear Tart:
1 cup sugar
2 cups water
3 pears
1 sheet puff pastry (from your grocer's freezer)
2 eggs
Fresh mint leaves for garnish (optional)

Preheat oven to 375°.

Heat sugar and water in medium saucepan. Core pears and cut in half lengthwise; simmer in sugar/water mixture until tender, remove and cool.

Cut puff pastry into pear shapes, approximately twice the size of the pears; place on greased cookie sheet. Ladle a tablespoon of Custard in center of each pastry base. Slice each pear lengthwise and fan out over Custard, allowing enough exposed pastry to puff around filling. Brush pastry with beaten egg mixture. Bake 8 to 10 minutes, until golden brown.

Place on plates, ladle Chocolate Sauce around the bottom of each tart. Garnish with mint leaves.

Custard:
1 cup heavy cream
6 egg yolks
1 tablespoon sugar
⅛ teaspoon vanilla extract

In small saucepan, heat cream to boiling, remove from heat.

Place egg yolks, sugar, and vanilla in mixing bowl (or top of double boiler), incorporate cream slowly so as not to scramble the eggs. Place mixture over boiling water and cook until thickened, stirring constantly (use a spoon, not a whisk). Remove from heat, chill quickly over ice, then refrigerate.

Chocolate Sauce:
½ cup heavy cream
8 ounces semisweet chocolate

Heat cream to boiling in a small saucepan. Chip chocolate into small pieces, place in mixing bowl. Pour boiling cream over the chocolate, stir until melted. Keep warm, but not over direct heat. ❧

Color Plate 21   The Wedding Day   Page 59
Tarrytown House Executive Conference Center

Fresh Maine Lobster Stuffed with Crabmeat and Shrimp, with Sauce Dijonnaise

COLOR PLATE 22   AN AMERICAN THANKSGIVING   PAGE 64
The American Club

L/R: Bourbon Caramel Apple Gratin, Hickory Smoked Wild Tom Turkey, Pear Pecan Barley, Whole Wheat Walnut Bread,
Tricolor Salad and Blue Cheese Soufflé, Great Lakes Chowder, Root Vegetable Julienne

COLOR PLATE 23   LUNCH FOR AN AUTUMN FOLIAGE TOUR   PAGE 67
The Equinox Hotel, Resort & Spa

L/R: Grilled Radicchio with Pickled Vegetables, Breast of Pheasant with Cranberries and Persimmons, Maple Potato Cakes,
Chestnut Corn Bread, Gingered Apple and Butternut Bisque, Pumpkin Cheesecake

Photography: John Rizzo, at Schnitzer Concert Hall

COLOR PLATE 24   AFTER THE THEATER   PAGE 70
The Heathman Hotel

Medallions of Veal with Forest Mushrooms and Whole-Grained Mustard, and Spaëtzle

COLOR PLATE 25   A DAY OF HORSEBACK RIDING   PAGE 73
The Homestead

French Venison Stew, with Späetzle

COLOR PLATE 26   TASTE OF THE SOUTH   PAGE 76
The Jefferson, a Grand Heritage Hotel

L/R: Crab and Corn Chowder, Oysters Jefferson,
Virginia Greens with Raspberry Vinaigrette, Loin of Lamb in Pastry

UNDER THE BLUE SKIES
Ojai Valley Inn & Country Club

Layered Veal Scallopini and Crispy Sweetbread

Photo: Robert Mitchell Photography

COLOR PLATE 28   THE MAINE EVENT   PAGE 82
Portland Regency Hotel

Baked Stuffed Maine Lobster with Shrimp and Scallops

UNDER THE BLUE SKIES

Ojai Valley Inn & Country Club
Ojai, California

*I*n 1923, Midwest glass manufacturing magnate Edward Drummond Libbey envisioned the development of the village of Ojai into "a renaissance of Spanish rural architecture in complete harmony with the land, the blue skies, and bright sunshine." Today, the keystone of his project, the Ojai Valley Inn & Country Club, continues its legacy as one of the nation's grand resorts.

Located just north of Los Angeles and nestled in the Topa Mountains a few miles inland from the Pacific Ocean, the inn is as well known for its spectacular setting, its legendary golf course—which annually hosts the Seniors PGA GTE West Classic—and its outstanding service and amenities. Chefs Yvan Lampron, Adalberto Rodarte, and Benoit Pepin invite you to experience another of the inn's hallmarks, its outstanding California-harvest cuisine.

Spiral of Smoked Salmon and Ahi Tuna Carpaccio

Baked Sea Scallops with Dungeness Crab Crust

Seared Lamb Loin
served with Flageolet Salad

Layered Veal Scallopini and Crispy Sweetbread

Red Flame Lamb Loin

Banana Fondue

COLOR PLATE 27

SPIRAL OF SMOKED SALMON AND
AHI TUNA CARPACCIO
Serves 6

12 ounces sushi grade Ahi tuna
1 cup extra virgin olive oil
Salt and pepper
1 bunch basil
12 ounces Scottish smoked salmon, thinly sliced
8 ounces arugula
⅓ cup fresh lemon juice
¼ cup capers
1 bunch chives, chopped

Slice the tuna ¼-inch thin and pound lightly to obtain same thickness as the salmon. Rest the tuna on plastic film. Brush with olive oil, salt and pepper to taste. Cover with the basil leaves. Place the sliced salmon on the above, roll the fish very tightly into the plastic and freeze for 2 hours.

To serve, slice the fish roll thinly and arrange on dinner plates. Place a bouquet of arugula in the center of each plate. Mix the olive oil and lemon juice and pour lightly over the fish and arugula. Sprinkle with capers and chives.

❧

BAKED SEA SCALLOPS
WITH DUNGENESS CRAB CRUST
Serves 6

4 slices egg bread
1 pound unsalted butter, softened
½ pound Dungeness crabmeat
½ bunch chives, chopped
½ bunch tarragon, chopped
Pinch cayenne pepper
18 jumbo sea scallops
Salt and pepper
1 bunch parsley
18 cocktail crab claws, cooked
Wild rice, for garnish

Preheat oven to 375º.
Trim bread and crumb in a food processor. Place crumbs in a bowl, add ¼ pound butter, crabmeat, chives, tarragon, and cayenne. Mix well.

Place the sea scallops in a baking dish, season with salt and pepper. Top generously with the crab mixture. Bake for 10 minutes, or until golden brown.

Meanwhile, cook parsley in boiling salted water for 2 minutes, strain. Using a blender, liquify the hot parsley with the remaining butter and a seasoning of salt and pepper.

Pour 3 dots of parsley butter the same size as the scallops on each plate; top with the scallops. Garnish each plate with 3 crab claws and wild rice.

SEARED LAMB LOIN
WITH FLAGEOLET SALAD
Serves 6

1 pound dry flageolet beans
1 garlic bulb
3 lamb loins, fat removed
2 bunches thyme, chopped
2 bunches rosemary, chopped
1 cup white wine
1 small onion, whole
3 slices bacon
1 bunch basil, chopped
½ cup fresh lemon juice
½ cup balsamic vinegar
3 cups extra virgin olive oil
Salt and pepper
Whole basil leaves and cracked black pepper, for garnish

Soak the flageolet beans in cold water for 1 hour.
Preheat oven to 450º.
Cut the garlic bulb in half lengthwise and rub ½ over the lamb loins. Sprinkle the loins with thyme and rosemary. Sear each loin in a hot pan for 2 minutes on each side. Finish in the oven for 4 minutes. Refrigerate lamb until completely cold.

Cook the flageolets in 3 cups water with the white wine, reserved ½ of garlic, whole onion, and bacon for 2 hours over low heat.

Strain the beans, reserving juice. Remove garlic, onion, and bacon. Add basil. Allow beans and juice to cool.

For dressing, mix ½ cup bean juice with lemon juice, vinegar, olive oil, and salt and pepper to taste. Mix vigorously, refrigerate.

To serve, mold the beans in the center of serving plates with a 4-inch ring. Slice the lamb loins paper thin and arrange on top of the beans. Drizzle with the vinaigrette dressing. Garnish with whole basil leaves and cracked pepper.

LAYERED VEAL SCALLOPINI
AND CRISPY SWEETBREAD
Serves 6

2 stalks celery
2 carrots
1 onion
2 bunches thyme
3 cloves garlic
Olive oil
1½ pounds veal sweetbread
1 cup white wine
1 cup port wine
3 cups veal stock
1 box phyllo dough
1 pound butter, melted
¼ cup truffle juice
Flour
6 5-inch veal scallopini

Roughly chop celery, carrots, onion, thyme, and garlic, sauté in a little olive oil. Add the sweetbread and white wine, cover, cook for 15 minutes over low heat. Add the port wine, reduce liquid by ½. Add the veal stock and cook gently for 2 hours. Reserving the sauce, remove sweetbread from the pan and remove skin, cut into 4-inch medallions.

Preheat oven to 375º.

Brush 3 sheets phyllo dough with butter, 1 at a time, and stack on one another. Use a 4-inch cookie cutter to cut 18 4-inch circles from the dough. Place the circles on a cookie sheet and bake until golden brown.

Strain the sauce and add the truffle juice. Bring to a boil and season to taste. Flour the veal on both sides, sauté in a hot pan with a little olive oil.

To serve, layer in sequence: 1 dough circle, a veal scallopini, sweetbread, then top with 1 dough circle. Drizzle with sauce. Garnish plate with fresh market vegetables.

RED FLAME LAMB LOIN
Serves 6

2 pounds red flame (seedless) grapes, stemmed
1 cup pinot noir
3 shallot bulbs, chopped
3 cups veal stock
Salt and pepper
1 cup bread crumbs
2 bunches fresh thyme, chopped
6 lamb loins
4 egg yolks
Oil

Liquify grapes in a blender, strain through a very fine strainer or cotton cloth. Reserve juice and pulp. Heat the grape juice in a small saucepan with the pinot noir and shallots, reduce until almost dry. Add the veal stock and reduce again by ½. Keep warm.

Mix grape pulp with bread crumbs and thyme. Brush loins with egg yolk, roll in crumb mixture to coat. Sauté the loins in a hot pan for 4 minutes on each side.

Pool sauce on serving plates, top with sliced lamb loin. Garnish with market vegetables.

❦

BANANA FONDUE
Serves 6

6 sheets phyllo dough
½ pound unsalted butter, melted
3 ripe bananas, sliced
¼ cup sugar
3 ounces semisweet chocolate shavings
1 can cream of coconut
½ cup heavy cream
¼ cup Myers's rum
¼ cup shredded coconut, roasted

Preheat oven to 350º.

Brush 1 sheet phyllo dough with butter. Lay a second sheet on the first and brush with butter. Repeat with third sheet. Follow the same procedure to create a second stack from the 3 remaining sheets. Use a pastry cutter to cut 12 4-inch circles from the phyllo dough. Place on a cookie sheet and bake for 10 minutes.

Place 6 of the baked circles on a smaller cookie sheet. Arrange sliced bananas on top. Sprinkle with sugar and place under a broiler for 1 to 2 minutes. Sprinkle the top with chocolate shavings and cover with 1 of the remaining phyllo dough circles.

Mix together the cream of coconut, heavy cream, and rum. Pour mixture on 6 dinner plates and top each with a banana fondue. Garnish with shredded coconut. ❧

THE MAINE EVENT

Portland Regency Hotel
Portland, Maine

*B*uilt in 1895 as an armory for the Maine National Guard, this Neo-Gothic Romanesque landmark retained its function until being decommissioned in the 1950s. Empty for some time, the building was purchased in 1984 for conversion into the Portland Regency Hotel.

Just two blocks from Portland's working waterfront, the Portland Regency is the centerpiece of the city's popular restored historic area, the Old Port Exchange. In addition to the architecturally distinctive hotel, visitors will find a charming neighborhood of shops, brick and cobblestone streets, and restaurants offering a wide variety of local dishes celebrating Maine's maritime heritage. The Portland Regency invites you to sample these simple to create, exceptionally flavorful, delightful contributions to American regional cooking.

Spicy Maine Crab Cakes
with Lemon Shallot Mayonnaise

Champagne Shrimp Bisque

Baked Stuffed Maine Lobster
with Shrimp and Scallops

New Potato and Tomato Pie

Asparagus with Orange Vinaigrette

Flaming Baked Acadia

COLOR PLATE 28

SPICY MAINE CRAB CAKES
Serves 4

1 pound fresh Maine crabmeat
1 cup bread crumbs, sifted
1 cup Ritz cracker crumbs, sifted
2 tablespoons onion, minced
1 egg, beaten
½ cup mayonnaise
Scant 2 tablespoons jalapeño peppers, chopped
2 teaspoons Worcestershire sauce
½ teaspoon salt
¼ teaspoon white pepper
Melted butter

Reserving a few tablespoons of bread and cracker crumbs, combine all ingredients until just blended. Do not overmix. Gently form into 2-ounce cakes, dust with reserved crumbs. Sauté in a little butter until browned on both sides. Serve with Lemon Shallot Mayonnaise.

LEMON SHALLOT MAYONNAISE
Yield, 1 cup

2 egg yolks
2 tablespoons lemon juice, freshly squeezed
1 teaspoon sugar
1 teaspoon dry mustard
¾ teaspoon salt
Dash white pepper
2 tablespoons shallots, minced
½ cup olive oil
½ cup salad oil

Put all ingredients except oils in a food processor. With the processor running, slowly add both oils until blended.

❧

CHAMPAGNE SHRIMP BISQUE
Serves 4

1 pound Maine shrimp
2 cups champagne
1 tablespoon pickling spices tied in cheesecloth
¼ cup cognac
1 cup cream
1 shallot, peeled
1 tablespoon butter

Peel and devein shrimp, poach in champagne with the bag of pickling spices for about 3 minutes. Strain liquid into a second saucepan. Add ½ of the cognac and the cream, reduce by almost ½. Puree the poached shrimp and the shallot, sauté in butter over medium-high heat for 1 minute. Add remaining cognac, flame. Return the mixture to the reserved liquid, serve.

❧

BAKED STUFFED MAINE LOBSTER WITH SHRIMP AND SCALLOPS

For each serving:
1 1¼-pound Maine lobster
6 Maine shrimp, peeled, deveined
4 Maine scallops
1 croissant
¼ cup cream
6 tablespoons butter, melted
2 tablespoons champagne

Preheat oven to 350°.
Lay live lobster on its back. Split with large knife from head to tail without cutting all the way through the body. Remove sack from inside near head. Remove entrails that are attached to the sack and lead all the way to the tail.
Cross-cut the tail 3 times, at top, middle, and end. Stuff with the uncooked shrimp and scallops. Chop croissant into small cubes and use it to fill the rest of the body cavity and tail. Drizzle with cream, butter, and champagne. Bake for 30 minutes.

❧

NEW POTATO AND TOMATO PIE
Serves 4

4 cups new potatoes, peeled, matchstick-cut
2 tomatoes, thinly sliced
1 small bunch basil leaves, cleaned, washed
2 teaspoons salt
2 teaspoons white pepper
¼ cup grated Parmesan cheese
½ stick butter, melted
Cherry tomatoes, for garnish

Preheat oven to 375°.
Soak the peeled and cut potatoes in cold water for 10 minutes, drain thoroughly. Spray a pie tin with nonstick coating. Layer potatoes, tomatoes, basil, salt, pepper, and Parmesan in pan. Drizzle with butter and bake for 1 to 1¼ hours.
Invert onto serving dish and cut into wedges. Garnish each with ½ a cherry tomato and broil for 2 minutes, if desired.

Fresh Asparagus
Serves 4

1 pound asparagus (green and purple)
1 cup champagne
Orange slices for garnish

Measure asparagus 5 inches from the tips and cut. Using your smallest diameter saucepan to allow the asparagus to stand while cooking, poach in champagne until tender but crisp. Chill immediately in ice water, then remove to drain.

Marinate in Orange Vinaigrette ½ hour before serving. Garnish with orange slices.

Orange Vinaigrette
Yield, about 1 ½ cups

1 orange, peeled, seeded, chopped
½ cup orange juice
½ teaspoon salt
¼ teaspoon pepper, freshly ground
½ teaspoon Dijon mustard
1 tablespoon fresh herbs (oregano, basil, thyme), chopped
¾ cup olive oil

Combine all ingredients and shake well.

Flaming Baked Acadia
Serves 4

Apple brownie:
1 cup sugar
1 stick margarine
1 egg
2 apples, chopped
⅓ cup walnuts, chopped
1 cup flour
½ teaspoon baking powder
½ teaspoon baking soda
¼ teaspoon salt
½ teaspoon cinnamon

Preheat oven to 350°.

Cream sugar into margarine. Mix in balance of ingredients and bake in a 7 x 11-inch pan for 40 minutes. Cool.

To serve:
Vanilla ice cream
8 egg whites at room temperature
2 cups confectioners' sugar, sifted
1 teaspoon vanilla extract
½ cup cognac

Line 4 soup cups with plastic wrap and chill. Cut the cooled brownies into squares that will fit into the inside edge of the cups. Scoop ice cream into bottom half of the cups and cover with the brownie squares. Freeze.

Prepare meringue by whipping egg whites until frothy. Add vanilla and sugar slowly, continuing to whip until stiff peaks form.

Preheat oven to 450°.

Unmold frozen desserts onto shallow baking dishes. Put meringue in a pastry bag with a star tip, encase each dessert entirely in meringue and bake until meringue is browned (the inside should remain frozen). At the table, straight from the oven, pour 2 tablespoons cognac on each dish and ignite. The cognac will burn for a few moments. ❧

TAKE ME OUT TO THE BALL GAME

Stouffer Tower City Plaza Hotel
Cleveland, Ohio

In 1815, Cleveland's first hotel, Mowrey's Tavern, opened on the site of today's Stouffer Tower City Plaza Hotel. Built as part of a master plan for a downtown railroad terminal, the original 1,000-room property opened December 16, 1918, boasting a 10-story atrium at its core. A white brick, neoclassical building, the hotel was designed in an "E" shape to allow maximum natural lighting in all rooms. Excellent craftsmanship distinguishes the hotel: the facade is embellished with multiple cast-stone details, balustrades, ornamentation, and bronze canopies. An ambitious $37-million renovation has returned the hotel to its original grandeur.

Cleveland is a city known for professional sports. Join Stouffer Tower City Plaza Hotel with this elegant menu for entertaining before or after the game.

Grilled Crab Corn Cakes
with Horseradish Tartare

Fresh Lobster Salad
served with Field Greens
and Asparagus with Lime Vinaigrette

Grilled Wild Mushrooms and Vegetable Salad
with Dill Vinaigrette

Roasted Chicken
served with Warm New Potato Salad

Hazelnut Brownies

COLOR PLATE 29

Grilled Crab Corn Cakes
Serves 6

6 slices white bread, crusts removed
2 cups milk
3 tablespoons clarified butter
3 shallots, minced
1 stalk celery, finely diced
½ cup whole kernel corn
2 egg yolks
Pinch white pepper
Pinch salt
½ teaspoon Old Bay seasoning
1 pound fresh or canned pasteurized crabmeat
½ cup white bread crumbs
4 tablespoons vegetable oil mixed with clarified butter

Soak the bread in the milk 2 to 3 minutes. Squeeze the bread with your hands to remove excess milk.

To a large pan add butter, shallots, and celery, sauté on medium heat until celery is soft, about 2 minutes. Add the corn and continue to sauté. Reduce heat to low, add soaked bread. Mix with a rubber spatula and bring to a slow boil. The mixture should look like dough.

Add egg yolks and seasonings. Remove from heat and gently fold in crabmeat. Divide into 6 portions and gently form into 3½-inch patties. Chill for 30 minutes.

Lightly sprinkle bread crumbs on tops and bottoms of patties. Brown patties for 1½ to 2 minutes on each side in a nonstick pan with a little vegetable oil and clarified butter. Serve with Horseradish Tartare.

Horseradish Tartare
Yield, about 1¼ cups

Blend together:
1 cup mayonnaise
1 tablespoon freshly grated or prepared horseradish, drained
½ tablespoon capers, chopped
½ tablespoon pickled cucumber, chopped
1 hard-boiled egg, chopped
1 tablespoon chives, chopped
1 teaspoon dry mustard
4 dashes Tabasco

Fresh Lobster Salad
with Field Greens and Asparagus
Serves 4

4 1½-pound Maine lobsters, poached in court bouillon, drained and cooled
Field Greens and Asparagus Salad
Lime Vinaigrette
2 oranges, sectioned, for garnish
1 red bell pepper, julienne, for garnish

Separate the claws and tails from the lobster body. Remove claw shells, split tails in halves, remove meat and reserve.

Toss the salad and arrange on plates. Top each salad with 2 claws and 2 halves of lobster tail. Drizzle each with Lime Vinaigrette. Garnish with orange sections and red pepper.

Salad:
12 asparagus spears, pencil thin
1 bunch curly endive
1 head Belgian endive, julienne
4 red oak lettuce leaves
2 bunches arugula

Cut 3 inches below the tips of the asparagus. Boil the tips in salted water for 1 minute, cool, and drain. Stem the greens and separate leaves. Toss the salad and arrange on 4 plates.

Lime Vinaigrette
Yield, about ¾ cup

Blend together:
¼ cup lime juice
½ cup olive oil
½ teaspoon salt
½ teaspoon dry mustard
Pinch black pepper

Grilled Wild Mushroom and Vegetable Salad
Serves 4

1 bulb fennel
1 yellow squash
1 zucchini
1 red bell pepper, stemmed, quartered
4 ounces stemless shiitake mushrooms
4 ounces stemless porcino mushrooms

Marinade:
4 shallots, minced
4 tablespoons balsamic vinegar
¼ cup vegetable oil
4 garlic cloves, chopped
1 bunch dill stems, chopped, leaves reserved

Slightly trim bottom of fennel. Cut bulb into 8 wedges, allowing leaves to remain intact. Cut squash and zucchini into ¼-inch pieces. Marinate all vegetables and mushrooms for 1 hour.
Prepare a hot grill.
Remove vegetables from marinade and grill approximately 10 seconds each. Sear each side of the mushrooms for 1 minute. Plate all vegetables and mushrooms, drizzle with Dill Vinaigrette

Dill Vinaigrette
Yield, about ½ cup

Mix together:
2 tablespoons balsamic vinegar
5 tablespoons olive oil
Pinch salt
½ teaspoon dry mustard
Reserved dill leaves (from above)

Roasted Chicken
Serves 6

1 6- to 7-pound roasting chicken, whole
2 tablespoons vegetable oil

For seasoning, mix:
1 tablespoon cumin
1 tablespoon salt
½ teaspoon white pepper
1 tablespoon rosemary, chopped

Preheat oven to 375º.
Cut off the chicken wings and tie legs to the back with string. Brush the chicken with vegetable oil and season generously with ¾ of the seasoning mix.
Place the chicken on its side in a roasting pan. Roast for 35 minutes, turn it on its other side, roast an additional 35 minutes, basting periodically with vegetable oil. Sprinkle with remaining seasoning before removing from the oven. Serve with Warm New Potato Salad.

Warm New Potato Salad
Serves 6

2 pounds new (red) potatoes

Boil with skin on until tender, drain, and cube. Toss lightly with sauce.
For sauce, blend:
4 minced shallots
¼ teaspoon white pepper
2 teaspoons dry mustard
¼ teaspoon salt
¼ cup olive oil
4 tablespoons cider vinegar
¾ cup hot chicken stock

Hazelnut Brownies
Serves 6

5 ounces unsweetened chocolate
½ cup unsalted butter, softened
2 whole eggs
2 egg whites
¾ cup sugar
Zest of 1 lemon
1 teaspoon vanilla extract
4 tablespoons honey
¾ cup all-purpose flour, sifted
Pinch salt
½ teaspoon baking powder
½ cup hazelnuts, chopped

Preheat oven to 350º.
Melt the chocolate over hot water, remove from heat, cool to room temperature. Mix in butter until dissolved. Separately, whip together eggs, egg whites, sugar, lemon zest, vanilla, and honey until fluffy. Fold in the chocolate mixture. Fold in balance of ingredients.
Pour batter into a greased 9-inch round or 8-inch square pan and bake for 30 minutes. Take care not to overcook. ∾

Go West
Strater Hotel
Durango, Colorado

After traveling over high Rocky Mountain passes or through the Painted Desert, guests like Will Rogers, John F. Kennedy, and Louis L'Amour arrived in Durango looking forward to a stay at the Strater Hotel. Built in 1887, this four-story, red brick hotel is 105 years old and, without a doubt, better than ever! The elegant Strater is the centerpiece of Durango's historic district, featuring 93 guest rooms furnished with authentic American Victorian walnut antiques, elaborate Bradbury and Bradbury wallpaper, heavy velvet drapes, and all the modern comforts.

Guests can visit cliff dwellings at Mesa Verde National Park, take a scenic train ride on the Durango/Silverton Narrow Gauge Railroad, participate in any of a host of enjoyable outdoor activities, or relax in the hotel's old west saloon.

Black Bean and Chorizo Soup
Fresh Green Salad
with Strawberry Vinaigrette

Coal Creek Chicken with Raspberry Coulis
Cream Cheese Brownies

COLOR PLATE 30

BLACK BEAN AND CHORIZO SOUP
Yield, 1 gallon

1 cup black beans, dry
5 quarts water
10 ounces chorizo (Mexican sausage), cooked
1½ tablespoons chicken base
2 tablespoons fresh cilantro, finely chopped
6 tablespoons roux (equal amounts flour and butter,
  cooked slightly)
½ cup heavy cream

Combine beans and 2 quarts water, boil 45 minutes. Puree chorizo and add to the beans. Boil an additional 30 minutes. Set aside, cool slightly. Puree mixture, strain, reserve beans and liquid.

Heat strained liquid with 3 quarts water. Add chicken base and cilantro. Bring to a boil and add roux, mix until dissolved. Strain again and add the liquid to the reserved bean mixture. Add cream, stir.

COAL CREEK CHICKEN

For each serving:
2 tablespoons blanched spinach
1 tablespoon unsalted butter
⅓ cup white wine
½ cup heavy cream
1 4-ounce breast of chicken, skinless
2 ounces chorizo (Mexican sausage), cooked, pureed
2 tablespoons pine nuts, toasted

Blanch spinach in steamer for 2 minutes. Drain and finely chop, then sauté spinach in butter for 1 minute. Add wine and reduce completely. Add cream and reduce by ½. Cool.

Pound chicken breast out into a flat sheet and cover with spinach mixture. Sprinkle with chorizo and pine nuts. Roll up and wrap with plastic wrap. Steam in the plastic wrap for 20 minutes. Remove from heat, remove plastic wrap. Slice into ½-inch slices and serve atop Raspberry Coulis.

RASPBERRY COULIS
Yield, 6 cups

1 quart frozen whole raspberries, thawed
1 tablespoon cumin
1 tablespoon garlic powder
2 cups sugar
1 tablespoon chicken base

Combine all ingredients and simmer for 30 minutes, stirring occasionally.

FRESH GREEN SALAD
Yield, variable

Create a simple salad with your choice of seasonal greens. Toss with Strawberry Vinaigrette.

STRAWBERRY VINAIGRETTE
Yield, about 3 cups

1 pint strawberries, hulled, halved
¼ cup red wine vinegar
3 tablespoons honey
2 cups olive oil
½ teaspoon black pepper

Puree strawberries, add vinegar and honey. Add oil slowly and season lightly with black pepper. Refrigerate at least 2 hours before serving.

CREAM CHEESE BROWNIES
Yield, 40 2-inch-square brownies

2½ cups unsalted butter
10 ounces semisweet chocolate
10 eggs
5½ cups sugar
2½ cups flour
2½ cups walnuts
4 teaspoons vanilla extract
14 ounces cream cheese
¼ cup cocoa
Parchment paper

Preheat oven to 300°.

Melt butter slowly over double boiler. Chop chocolate into small pieces and add to the butter, stirring until melted. Remove from heat.

Mix 7 eggs and 4¼ cups of sugar until smooth. Add chocolate mixture. Add flour and mix thoroughly. Add nuts and 2 teaspoons vanilla.

Spray and flour 2 9 x 13-inch baking pans, line with parchment paper. Fill with chocolate mixture.

Mix cream cheese until smooth. Add remaining sugar and the cocoa, then remaining eggs 1 at a time. Add remaining vanilla. Swirl cream cheese mixture into the chocolate mixture. Bake for approximately 1 hour.

An Art Museum Tour

The Tutwiler, a Camberley Hotel
Birmingham, Alabama

*F*rom its opening in 1914, the original Tutwiler was *the* premier gathering place for Alabama's business and civic leaders, and host to all visiting celebrities. In 1974, the hotel gained final notoriety by becoming the first high-rise to be demolished by implosion. Recreated by renovation of one of Birmingham's most prominent addresses—the Ridgely Apartment Hotel — the new Tutwiler opened in 1986.

Built by Edward Magruder Tutwiler in 1913, the Ridgely's fine Italianate architectural details provide an ambience for today's Tutwiler equal to its predecessor. Elegantly furnished, the hotel houses a unique collection of art, including paintings on loan from the city's Museum of the Arts. Central to the city's cultural district, the Tutwiler is a popular destination for arts patrons. The Tutwiler's chef, Michael Clavelin, captures the essence of an afternoon with the arts in the following elegant menu.

Timbale of Partridge a L'ancienne
Fillet of Dover Sole au Sauternes
Lime Sherbet
Fillet of Bison au Poivre Noir
Pomegranate Soufflé, Oriental

COLOR PLATE 31

TIMBALE OF PARTRIDGE A L'ANCIENNE
Serves 6

2 medium partridges, deboned, bones reserved
4 egg whites
⅓ cup whipping cream
Salt, pepper, dash nutmeg

Sauce:
½ cup butter
2 carrots, diced
¼ cup celery, diced
1 medium onion, medium-fine chopped
1 bay leaf
1 branch thyme
½ cup tomato paste
1 cup all-purpose flour
2 quarts chicken stock
¾ cup dry white wine
2 tablespoons cognac
¼ cup Madeira wine

Puree partridge. Beat the egg whites into a stiff froth and add to the meat mixture. Incorporate the cream very slowly. Add salt, pepper, and nutmeg.

Preheat oven to 375°.

Butter 6 8-ounce ramekins and fill to ¾ with the mixture. Bake for 20 minutes in a water bath.

Sauce:

Preheat a large skillet with 4 tablespoons butter. Add the partridge bones, carrots, celery, onion, bay leaves, and thyme. Sauté until golden brown. Add the tomato paste and flour. When the mix becomes a paste, pour in the chicken stock, add white wine, cook slowly for about 35 minutes.

Strain the sauce through a fine strainer. Put the sauce back on the stove and boil for 5 minutes. Add cognac, Madeira, and 4 tablespoons butter. Serve over partridge.

❧

FILLET OF BISON AU POIVRE NOIR
Serves 6

1 whole bison (buffalo) tenderloin
⅓ cup black peppercorns, coarsely crushed
½ cup butter
⅓ cup Armagnac or cognac
1½ cups brown sauce

Trim the tenderloin, remove silver skin and tail. Roll the fillet in the crushed peppercorns until it is completely crusted. Place fillet and butter in a saucepan and cook over medium heat for 25 minutes. Keep turning the fillet to cook on all sides. When the fillet is cooked to medium rare, pour in the liquor and ignite. After the alcohol has burned off, add the brown sauce and simmer for 10 minutes. Remove the tenderloin and slice into 6 portions.

Bring the sauce to preferred consistency by reduction and pour over fillet. Serve with your favorite vegetable and potatoes.

FILLET OF DOVER SOLE AU SAUTERNES
Serves 6

½ cup butter
⅓ cup shallots, finely chopped
Branch of fresh thyme
3 18- to 20-ounce Dover sole, filleted, bones reserved
¾ cup Sauternes
¾ cup heavy cream
Juice of ½ lemon

In a large saucepan, melt ½ the butter, add the chopped shallots, thyme, and fish bones which have been cut into pieces. Sauté for 10 minutes over low fire, do not brown. Add the Sauternes and reduce by ½. Add the cream. Bring to a boil, strain.

In another pan, place the fillet of sole and cover with the sauce. Poach for 7 to 8 minutes. Place sole on a tray and keep warm. Reduce the sauce to a creamy consistency, add the remaining butter and the lemon juice. Pour over the sole.

❧

POMEGRANATE SOUFFLÉ, ORIENTAL
Serves 6

1 cup flour
1 cup sugar
4 eggs plus 3 egg yolks
1 quart milk
Vanilla extract
½ cup butter
5 egg yolks
12 egg whites
Lady fingers
Grenadine syrup
Kirschwasser
Spun sugar
Small candies

Preheat oven to 350°.

Thoroughly mix flour, sugar, eggs, and yolks in a saucepan. Gradually add boiling milk. Add a few drops of vanilla extract and boil. Cook 5 minutes stirring constantly. Remove from stove. Add butter, 5 egg yolks, and 12 egg whites, having beaten the whites to a stiff froth.

Arrange soufflé in layers in a timbale alternating sponge lady fingers saturated with grenadine and Kirschwasser, and the soufflé.

Bake 20 minutes.

On taking the soufflé from the oven, cover with a veil of spun sugar and sprinkle the soufflé with small candies (flavored with grenadine) to look like pomegranate seeds. ❧

WINTER

A Delta Queen Holiday Dinner

The Delta Queen
New Orleans, Louisiana

*L*isted in the National Register of Historic Places and designated a National Historic Landmark, the *Delta Queen* is a survivor, a legend, and the last of her kind—an authentic, fully restored overnight paddle wheel steamboat. Built in 1926, she carries passengers on luxury river cruises through America's heartland.

Much like the scenery, musical entertainment, history, and heritage enjoyed by her passengers, the cuisine aboard the *Delta Queen* reflects the bounty and variety of the American experience. The *Delta Queen* cruises out of New Orleans, and many items on her menu derive from the city's Creole and Cajun culinary heritage. The following menu might be adopted for the December holiday season, when Southern—and Steamboatin'—hospitality abounds.

Blackened Sirloin with Creole Mustard Sauce

Crawfish en Croûte

Minnesota Wild Rice Soup

Spinach Salad
with Duck and Andouille Dressing

Veal Nottoway
with Artichokes, Crabmeat,
Creole Hollandaise, and Sweet Peppers

Crabmeat Stuffed Catfish
with Cajun Beurre Blanc

Mississippi Mud Pie

Kahlúa Crêpes

COLOR PLATE 32

Continued, page 95

COLOR PLATE 29   TAKE ME OUT TO THE BALL GAME   PAGE 85
Stouffer Tower City Plaza Hotel

L/R: Fresh Lobster Salad with Field Greens and Asparagus with Lime Vinaigrette,
Roasted Chicken with Warm New Potato Salad

Photography: MARONA

COLOR PLATE 30   GO WEST   PAGE 88
Strater Hotel

Coal Creek Chicken with Raspberry Coulis

Photography: Bob Silor

L/R: Timbale of Partridge a L'ancienne, Fillet of Dover Sole au Sauternes,
Pomegranate Souffle Oriental, Fillet of Bison au Poivre Noir

Photography: Syndey Byrd

COLOR PLATE 32   STEAMBOATIN'—A DELTA QUEEN HOLIDAY DINNER   PAGE 94
The Delta Queen

L/R: Kahlúa Crepes, Mississippi Mud Pie

COLOR PLATE 33   A WINE MAKER'S DINNER   PAGE 97
El Encanto Hotel and Garden Villas

Garlic-Grilled Santa Barbara Spot Prawns

COLOR PLATE 34   VALENTINE'S DAY   PAGE 100
The Hotel Hershey

L/R: Lancaster County Spring Lamb Rack for Two with Old English Mint Sauce, Hotel Hershey
Bouquetiere of Vegetables, Hershey Charlotte with English Apricot Sauce

MERRY CHRISTMAS
The Red Lion Inn

L/R: Red Lion Chocolate Chip Pie, Roast Goose with Orange Gravy and Apple-Apricot Chestnut Stuffing, Baked Stuffed
Potatoes, Vegetable Bundles, Cream of Tomato and Cheddar Soup

Photo: Vano Photography

HAPPY NEW YEAR!
The Westin St. Francis

Clockwise from Top: Chocolate Crème Brûlée, Salad Medley with Lemon Sherry Dressing, Rack of Lamb with Saffron
Couscous and Minted Cranberry-Orange Relish, Fillet of Trout with Caviar Beurre Blanc

Blackened Sirloin
Serves 6

2 pound center prime sirloin of beef
½ cup vegetable oil
Blackened Seasoning
1 stick butter, patted
Red onion and capers, for garnish

Preheat oven to 350°.

Trim fat to ⅛ inch on sirloin, coat with oil, and dredge completely with seasoning. Place sirloin in a hot iron skillet. Add 2 to 3 pats butter. Cook 5 minutes on each side, adding butter as needed. Transfer to oven and roast until internal temperature reaches 115°. Remove, refrigerate overnight.

To serve, slice sirloin into 12 even pieces and arrange on a chilled plate. Serve with a ¼ cup pool of Creole Mustard Sauce, garnish with chopped onion and capers.

Blackened Seasoning
Yield, 1 cup

Mix well:
⅓ cup paprika
1 tablespoon each white, black, and cayenne pepper
½ teaspoon each dried thyme, basil, and oregano
¼ cup salt

Creole Mustard Sauce
Yield, approximately 1 cup

1 cup Creole mustard
2 tablespoons mayonnaise
1 tablespoon Worcestershire sauce
1 teaspoon fresh ground black pepper

Blend the ingredients, chill.

❦

Crawfish en Croûte
Serves 6

2 tablespoons butter
1½ pounds crawfish tails, shelled
1 tablespoon each brandy and sherry
1½ cups heavy cream
1 tablespoon Blackened Seasoning
2 8 x 10-inch sheets puff pastry dough
1 egg mixed with 1 tablespoon water, for egg wash
Lemon wedges and parsley, for garnish

Melt butter over medium heat. Add crawfish tails and sauté 2 minutes. Deglaze with brandy and sherry; add cream and spices, reduce by ½. Preheat oven to 375°.

Water-wash the top of 1 layer of pastry dough. Place second sheet on top and cut 6 2½-inch diameter circles. Place on a cookie sheet and egg wash tops. Bake until puffed and golden brown. Serve each topped with 4 ounces crawfish, with sauce over the top. Garnish with lemon wedges and parsley.

Minnesota Wild Rice Soup
Serves 8

½ pound smoked bacon
1 each red, yellow, and green bell peppers, medium diced
1 large yellow onion, medium diced
2 ribs celery, small diced
1½ cups carrots, finely diced
2 garlic cloves, crushed
1 tablespoon fresh basil, finely diced
1½ teaspoons thyme
1 bay leaf
2 quarts chicken stock
½ pound wild rice
1 pound butter
1 cup flour
1 cup heavy cream
1 tablespoon Worcestershire sauce
1 tablespoon Tabasco
Salt and pepper

In a large soup pot, render bacon and sauté until crisp. Add vegetables and herbs, sweat for 15 minutes. Add stock and simmer ½ hour. Add rice and simmer 1 hour.

In separate pan, melt ½ the butter and add flour, cook 10 minutes over low heat to make roux. Add roux to soup and cook 15 minutes. Add heavy cream and finish with balance of butter, Worcestershire, and Tabasco; salt and pepper to taste.

❦

Spinach Salad with Duck and Andouille Dressing
Serves 6 to 8

2 duck breasts (12 ounces total)
Salt and pepper
1½ cups water
½ pound Andouille sausage
¼ cup red onion, diced
3 cloves garlic, crushed
1 cup red wine
1 teaspoon each basil, thyme, and oregano
½ cup red wine vinegar
1¼ cups vegetable oil
2 pounds fresh spinach
½ pound shiitake mushrooms, thinly sliced
½ pound feta cheese, ¼-inch diced

Preheat oven to 350°.

Season duck with salt and pepper. Oven-brown in a pan for 20 to 30 minutes, until well cooked; pour off grease. Add water and cover, simmer in oven for 1 to 1½ hours until duck is tender. Remove from pan, reserve stock. Remove skin from breasts, ½-inch dice.

(Continued, page 96.)

Over medium-high heat, sauté sausage in 2 table-spoons duck fat until browned. Add onion and garlic, cook until onions are clear. Add wine, reserved duck stock and herbs, reduce to ¼ liquid. Add duck breast and mix well, remove from heat. Add vinegar and whip in the oil. Keep warm over low heat.

Clean and wash spinach, drain well. Separate onto 6 to 8 salad plates, top each with equal amounts of mush-rooms and cheese. Serve with a generous ¼ cup of the warm dressing.

VEAL NOTTOWAY
Serves 6

1 3½-pound veal rack
Salt and pepper
2 cloves garlic, split lengthwise
2 tablespoons vegetable oil
12 to 16 artichoke hearts, halved
1 tablespoon butter
1 each red and yellow bell peppers, julienne
1 pound jumbo lump crabmeat, cleaned
Creole Hollandaise

Preheat oven to 350°.

Trim veal rack of excess fat and French the bones. Rub outside with salt, pepper, and garlic, brown in oil in a heavy skillet on all sides. Finish in oven to an internal temperature of 125° (medium rare). Remove from oven, let rest 20 minutes prior to serving.

Sauté artichoke hearts in butter, add pepper, and cook until tender but crisp. Add crabmeat and heat carefully, not breaking crab.

Carve veal rack, 1 bone per serving. Top with equal portions of vegetables and crab, finish with 2 tablespoons Creole Hollandaise.

CREOLE HOLLANDAISE
Yield, about 3 cups

8 egg yolks
1 tablespoon water
1 teaspoon Tabasco
1 tablespoon Creole mustard
1 tablespoon lemon juice
1¼ pounds butter, melted, clarified
Salt and cayenne pepper

Over double boiler, whip egg yolks, water, Tabasco, mustard, and lemon juice until mixture reaches soft peaks. Remove from heat. Slowly drizzle butter while whipping continuously until incorporated. Adjust season-ing with salt and pepper. Hold at room temperature.

CRABMEAT STUFFED CATFISH
Serves 6

Stuffing:

1 loaf cornbread, 3 x 6 x 1-inches, crumbled
½ pound jumbo lump crabmeat
1 cup cooked spinach, chopped
¼ cup pine nuts, toasted
1 tablespoon Creole mustard

Mix together cornbread, crabmeat, spinach, pine nuts, and mustard.

6 6-ounce boneless catfish fillets
Salt and pepper

Lay fish skin-side up and top with 2½ ounces stuffing. Roll tightly and refrigerate until set.

To finish:
1 cup seasoned flour
1 cup buttermilk
2 cups Zatarain* fish fry mix
Oil, for deep frying
Lemon wedges, for garnish

Preheat oven to 350°; heat frying oil to hot (350°).

Dredge rolled fish in seasoned flour, dip in buttermilk, and roll through fish fry mix. Deep fry until light brown. Remove to sheet pan and finish in oven to an internal temperature of 150°. Top each serving with 3 tablespoons Cajun Beurre Blanc, garnish with lemon.

*Not available locally? Write: Zatarain, Inc., 82 1st Street, P.O. Box 347, Gretna, LA 70053.

CAJUN BEURRE BLANC
Yield, 2½ cups

1½ cups white wine
1 fresh lemon, halved, squeezed
1 clove garlic, crushed
2 shallots, minced
1 teaspoon black peppercorns, cracked
1 bay leaf
1 cup heavy cream
1 pound butter, 1-inch patted
1 tablespoon Blackened Seasoning

Over low heat, combine first 6 ingredients, reduce by ½. Add heavy cream and reduce by ½. Slowly add butter, whipping continuously, alternating pan on and off the heat. Strain, stir in seasoning.

MISSISSIPPI MUD PIE
page 115

KUHLÚA CRÊPES
page 115

A Wine Maker's Dinner

El Encanto Hotel and Garden Villas
Santa Barbara, California

Overlooking Santa Barbara's red-tile roofs, the Pacific Ocean, and Channel Islands, El Encanto Hotel has been "essential Santa Barbara" for over 75 years. El Encanto became a premier California retreat early this century by catering to the East Coast carriage trade who spent much time enjoying the comfortable cottages and lush gardens.

The charm of El Encanto and Santa Barbara is matched by wines produced in the nearby Santa Ynez valleys. In January and February, warm sunny days give way to a slight chill in the air that Santa Barbarans call winter. These are perfect conditions for a Wine Maker's Dinner, usually a wine tasting and reception of hors d'oeuvres, followed by a dinner that carefully pairs local wines and Chef James Sly's New Traditional cuisine.

Garlic-Grilled Santa Barbara Spot Prawns

A Petit Bouillabaisse of Santa Barbara Mussels
with Rouille and Garlic Croutons

Brander Chardonnay 1989 Tête de Cuvée,
Santa Ynez Valley

A Salad of Baked Eureka Goat Cheese
with Seasonal Greens and Lettuces,
Hazelnut Dressing

Brander Sauvignon Blanc 1989 Tête de Cuvée, Santa Ynez Valley

Roast Rack of Venison au jus
with Pan Roasted Baby Fennel
and Truffled Cabbage Ravioli

Brander Bouchet 1989, Santa Ynez Valley

El Encanto Floating Islands

COLOR PLATE 33

Garlic-Grilled Santa Barbara Spot Prawns
Serves 4

12 jumbo Santa Barbara (10 to a pound) spot prawns,
  or shrimp
1 tablespoon garlic, chopped
4 tablespoons Santa Barbara extra virgin olive oil
Salt and ground pepper to taste
6 tablespoons Santa Barbara extra virgin olive oil
2 limes, halved, for garnish

Peel the shells from the prawns, retaining tails, devein. Marinate the prawns in garlic and 4 tablespoons olive oil, cover and refrigerate for at least 2 hours, preferably overnight.

Preheat grill to very hot. Season prawns with salt and pepper. Grill quickly on each side, taking care not to overcook. (Prawns are done when they just turn opaque and lose translucency.) Place 3 prawns on bed of Cucumber and Cilantro Salad on each plate.

Drizzle 6 tablespoons olive oil over prawns, garnish with limes.

Cucumber and Cilantro Salad
Serves 4

3 tablespoons sherry vinegar
6 tablespoons Santa Barbara extra virgin olive oil
Salt and fresh-ground pepper
½ medium cucumber, hothouse or European (seedless)
1 small bunch fresh cilantro

In a small bowl, mix vinegar and olive oil, season with salt and pepper. Slice cucumber in thin rounds. Pluck the individual leaves of cilantro and toss with the cucumbers and dressing. Divide the salad into 4 portions and place on center of each plate.

❧

A Petit Bouillabaisse of Mussels with Rouille and Garlic Croutons
Serves 8

For 2 quarts bouillabaisse stock:
2 pounds fish bones
¼ cup olive oil
¼ pound fennel, sliced
¼ pound onions, sliced
2 stalks celery, sliced
9 cloves (2 tablespoons) garlic, chopped
⅓ bunch thyme
1 bay leaf
1 tablespoon chopped basil
2 tablespoons tomato paste
1 quart fish stock
1 quart water, or shrimp stock
½ teaspoon cayenne pepper

Select bones from firm-fleshed fish: halibut, sea bass, or snapper (do not use tuna or mackerel bones). In a large

heated roasting pan, heat olive oil until smoking hot; add fish bones, brown lightly. Remove to large pot.

Add balance of ingredients, bring to boil, reduce heat and simmer 45 minutes—do not allow bottom to burn. Strain into a plastic or other nonreactive container.

For 2 quarts bouillabaisse soup:
¼ cup olive oil
2½ cups fennel, julienne
2½ cups onion, julienne
2½ cups celery, julienne
2½ cups leeks, julienne
Salt and fresh-ground pepper
¼ bunch thyme
2 generous dashes saffron
Peel of ¼ orange, dried, shredded
2 quarts bouillabaisse stock
½ russet potato, peeled, thinly sliced

Heat olive oil in large, thick-bottomed pot; sauté fennel, onion, celery, and leeks until tender. Season with salt and pepper to taste, add thyme, saffron, and dried orange peel. When vegetables are translucent, add bouillabaisse stock and simmer 20 minutes; add potato and simmer until cooked, adjust seasonings.

The bouillabaisse may be prepared ahead up to this point, and refrigerated up to the point of cooking and serving.

To finish:
40 mussels
2 quarts bouillabaisse soup
1 cup Brander sauvignon blanc
¼ cup chopped Italian parsley
8 slices Sly Bread or French bread, fried in olive oil
Rouille

Clean mussels to remove beards, set aside.

Bring the soup to a boil in a wide, thick-bottomed pot. Add sauvignon blanc, bring to simmer, add the mussels. After 2 minutes, return to a boil over high heat. Reduce to a simmer and cook until mussels just open—discard any that are not.

Ladle bouillabaisse into large serving bowl or individual bowls, sprinkle with chopped parsley. Spread Rouille on bread or stir into broth as desired.

❧

Sly Bread
page 111

ROUILLE
Yield, 3 Cups

2 tablespoons russet potato, boiled
2 egg yolks
1 tablespoon garlic, finely chopped
1 teaspoon lemon juice
1 teaspoon paprika
⅓ teaspoon cayenne pepper
⅓ teaspoon salt
Pinch saffron or roasted saffron threads
¾ cup extra virgin olive oil
2 tablespoons hot water

All ingredients should be at room temperature. Force potato through a sieve into a bowl or food processor. Add egg yolks, garlic, lemon juice, paprika, cayenne, salt, and saffron, whisk or lightly process to combine. Gradually add olive oil in thin stream, blending until incorporated and fully emulsified, add water.

BAKED GOAT CHEESE SALAD
Serves 6

1 12-ounce goat cheese log
½ cup hazelnut oil
3 slices Sly Bread or French bread
Butter and olive oil
2 cloves garlic, peeled
Seasoned bread crumbs
6 2-ounce portions mixed baby salad greens
¾ cup Hazelnut Dressing
Freshly ground black pepper

Cut the goat cheese into 2-ounce rounds, marinate in hazelnut oil, turning to coat all sides.

Preheat oven to 450°.

Soak bread slices in a 50/50 mixture of melted butter and olive oil, bake until golden brown, turning once. When cooled, rub with garlic cloves to season, crumble into small croutons.

To serve, remove cheese from oil, roll in bread crumbs and bake at 450° for 6 to 8 minutes, until crumbs are golden brown. Meanwhile, toss greens with Hazelnut Dressing, season with pepper to taste.

Place greens on serving plates, use a spatula to top with baked cheese; add croutons, serve immediately.

HAZELNUT DRESSING
Yield, 1½ cups

½ shallot, thinly sliced
½ cup sherry vinegar
1 cup hazelnut oil
¼ teaspoon salt
Fresh ground black pepper to taste

Puree all ingredients in a blender, adjust seasonings with salt and pepper.

ROAST RACK OF VENISON AU JUS
Serves 8

Salted water for blanching
8 baby fennel (sweet anise)
1 8-rib venison rack, trimmed, tied
Salt and freshly ground black pepper
½ cup corn oil
3 cups brown stock (venison or veal)
¼ cup shallots, chopped
1½ cups dry red wine
(Optional) arrowroot and ½ cup butter to thicken sauce

Use venison trimmings to create stock, or use prepared veal stock.

Bring salted water to a boil, blanch fennel 5 minutes, drain, let cool.

Preheat oven to 350°.

Season venison rack heavily with salt and pepper. Heat oil in a heavy pan, carefully brown the rack on all sides. Place the fennel around the roast and brown lightly. Add 1 cup stock and place rack in oven, turning occasionally, until the roast reaches an internal temperature of 130°. (Remove the fennel earlier if it is getting too brown.) Keep pan moist with small amounts of water—do not let stock boil away. When done, remove roast and fennel from pan, keep warm on a platter.

For au jus, put pan over high heat, degrease, add the chopped shallots and wine. Reduce until syrupy. Add remaining stock, simmer 5 minutes, season to taste (should stock be thin, thicken with arrowroot and butter), strain. Drizzle au jus over Truffled Cabbage Ravioli. Carve roast and serve.

TRUFFLED CABBAGE RAVIOLI
page 111

PROVENÇAL RAVIOLI DOUGH
page 111

EL ENCANTO FLOATING ISLANDS
page 112

CRÈME ANGLAISE
page 112

VALENTINE'S DAY
The Hotel Hershey
Hershey, Pennsylvania

The Hotel Hershey is the legacy of chocolate magnate Milton Hershey, whose "great building campaign" was designed to employ the town's construction workers during the Depression. Completed in 1933, it is styled after the famous 19th-century grand hotels of the Mediterranean. Its noted architecture features a Spanish-influenced galleried lobby with a hand-sculpted fountain, tiled floors, and a wide, oak-railed mezzanine. Some public rooms include stained-glass windows, many offering vistas of the 20 acres of manicured formal gardens, reflecting pools, and fountains. Of note, the famed Circular Dining Room has been a favorite destination for romantic dining for generations.

Chicken Mole Alumette
with Supreme Sauce

Champagne and Scallop Chowder

Lancaster County Spring Lamb Rack for Two
with Old English Mint Sauce
and Hotel Hershey Bouquetiere

Tricolor Salad
with Hershey's Dressing

Hershey Charlotte
with English Apricot Sauce

COLOR PLATE 34

CHICKEN MOLE ALUMETTE
Serves 2

2 boneless chicken breasts, skins removed
Olive oil
1 small onion, diced
1 green bell pepper, diced
1 red bell pepper, diced
1 chili pepper (any variety), diced
2 tablespoons chili powder
½ tablespoon cumin
4 tablespoons cocoa
Juice and zest of 2 limes
1 clove garlic, minced
½ cup crème de cacao
2 cups chicken stock
Approximately 8 ounces puff pastry
1 egg beaten with 1 tablespoon water, for egg wash

Sear the chicken in the olive oil, remove, set aside. Toss the onion and peppers in the hot skillet, add balance of ingredients except crème de cacao and chicken stock. Reduce heat to low, cook thoroughly until vegetables are tender. Deglaze pan with the liqueur, add chicken stock, return breasts to the pan, cover, cook over low heat until chicken is very tender, about 30 minutes.

Remove chicken, dice finely, reserve. Place entire contents of the pan in a food processor, puree until smooth. Add the diced chicken.

Preheat oven to 325°.

Prepare the puff pastry by rolling it to a thickness of approximately ⅛ inch. Cut into 2 rectangles 4 inches wide and 12 inches long. Egg wash both surfaces, place chicken mixture in a strip on 1 of the pastry rectangles, leaving a ½-inch border. Top with the other pastry to form a lid, and seal edges with the tines of a fork. Vent the lid by piercing with a fork at ½-inch intervals. Bake for approximately 30 minutes. Serve with Supreme Sauce.

SUPREME SAUCE
Yield, variable

Thicken a good quality chicken stock with a mix of water and cornstarch, salt and pepper to taste. If desired, finish with a bit of cream and a tablespoon of butter.

CHAMPAGNE AND SCALLOP CHOWDER
Serves 8 to 10

1 pound bay scallops
2½ quarts water
2 leeks (white portion only), 1 diced, 1 rough cut
6 medium mushrooms, rough cut
½ of 1 bunch parsley stems
1 celery rib, rough cut
3 sprigs fresh or 1 tablespoon dried thyme
2 bay leaves
1 tablespoon black peppercorns
1 cup semidry champagne
1 cup heavy cream, or evaporated milk
Salt and white pepper

Plunge the scallops into the boiling water, remove after 1 minute, set aside.

Place all rough cut vegetables and herbs into the water, lower the heat and simmer for about 2 hours. Strain the stock to remove the vegetables and herbs. Sauté the diced leek, deglaze with the champagne. When the champagne reaches a boil, add to the simmering stock. Return the scallops to the stock, thicken with a mix of cornstarch and cold water or a roux of butter and flour. Allow the soup to simmer for about ½ hour, stir in the cream, season to taste with salt and white pepper.

LANCASTER COUNTY SPRING LAMB RACK FOR TWO

1 8-bone lamb rack, well trimmed
Cooking oil
Salt/Herb Seasoning (page 102)
¼ cup Dijon mustard
2 cups fresh bread crumbs
2 tablespoons fresh parsley, chopped
2 tablespoons fresh chives, chopped

Sear the surface of the lamb rack in a very hot pan with a small amount of cooking oil. Sprinkle the surface of the rack with the Salt/Herb Seasoning, coat with Dijon mustard. Dredge in the bread crumbs, which have been mixed with the parsley and chives.

Preheat oven to 350°.

Place the lamb rack in the preheated oven. Roast until done to desired finish. Check with an internal meat thermometer to assure doneness.

Approximately 10 minutes before the lamb is done, place the serving platter with the vegetables in the oven. Center the rack in the platter to carve and serve.

SALT/HERB SEASONING
Yield, variable

1 part salt
½ part white pepper
½ part black pepper
1 part garlic powder
1 part rosemary leaves, crushed
½ part thyme leaves
¼ part basil
¼ part oregano
¼ part marjoram
¼ part paprika

This seasoning mixture can be made in any quantity and reserved for later use.

HOTEL HERSHEY BOUQUETIERE
Yield, variable

2 tomato cups, hollowed:
filled with yellow squash and zucchini, Parisienne cut (melon scoop).
1 onion, thinly sliced:
to place under lamb rack.
Potatoes, mushroom cut:
Insert an apple corer ½ way into the potato; insert paring knife perpendicular to the to the corer, turn the potato, carefully remove the corer. The potatoes may be steamed or fried.
Premier (baby) carrots, bit of green attached:
peeled and steamed.
Mushrooms, lightly sautéed:
served in bouchées or pastry shells (available from specialty food stores).
Green beans, quickly blanched:
bundled in bacon, which has been half cooked then rolled around the beans.

Arrange all of the above on the serving platter, allowing space in the center for the lamb rack. Place the platter in the oven with the lamb 10 minutes before the lamb is done.

OLD ENGLISH MINT SAUCE
Yield, 2 cups

¾ cup granulated sugar
1½ cups water
1 cup apple cider vinegar
1 tablespoon shallots, chopped
2 mint tea bags
Salt and pepper
Cornstarch or arrowroot (optional)

Combine the sugar and ½ cup water in a saucepan over high heat, cook until the sugar is dark brown in color, but not burned. While stirring, slowly add the balance of water, and vinegar (the sugar will spatter if the liquid is not added slowly). Add the shallots, open the tea bags and add the mint leaves, salt and pepper to taste. Simmer for ½ hour. The sauce is ready to serve, or it may be thickened with a bit of cornstarch or arrowroot dissolved in water.

❧

TRICOLOR SALAD
Serves 6 to 8

1 head red oak lettuce
2 heads Belgian endive
3 bunches mâche
2 large tomatoes, peeled, seeded
10 radishes, shredded

Arrange on serving plates, serve with Hershey's Dressing.

HERSHEY'S DRESSING
Yield, 3 cups

¼ cup Dijon mustard
¼ cup red wine vinegar
2 tablespoons black pepper, crushed
1 teaspoon garlic, chopped
2 cups mayonnaise
2 tablespoons chives, chopped
Worcestershire sauce, salt, and sugar to taste

Combine all the ingredients in a mixing bowl and whisk until combined. Chill well, serve. ✑

HERSHEY CHARLOTTE
page 116

ENGLISH APRICOT SAUCE
page 116

AMERETTI COOKIES
page 116

Merry Christmas

The Red Lion Inn
Stockbridge, Massachusetts

*F*irst a stagecoach stop in 1773, then rebuilt in 1897, the Red Lion is one of the few American inns in use since the 18th century. "The hotel ... is a graceful structure in the colonial style, simple yet elegant and appointed after the luxurious fashion of a gentleman's country house. 'Inn' is a modest title for this ... hotel, but well indicates the nature of the cordial hospitality offered ...." This review, from an 1897 newspaper article, applies perfectly today.

Immortalized in Norman Rockwell's painting *Mainstreet, Stockbridge,* the inn, filled with a fine collection of Staffordshire china, colonial pewter, and 18th-century furnishings, epitomizes New England charm. An old-fashioned Christmas dinner with all the trimmings here provides armchair travelers a perfect taste of the inn's delightful hospitality.

Cream of Tomato and Cheddar Soup
Roast Goose with Orange Gravy
Apple-Apricot Chestnut Dressing
Baked Stuffed Potato Red Lion
Vegetable Bundles
Red Lion Inn Chocolate Chip Pie

COLOR PLATE 35

CREAM OF TOMATO AND CHEDDAR SOUP
12 Servings

1 small onion
4 stalks celery, leaves removed
3 carrots, peeled
4 tablespoons extra virgin olive oil
2 pounds canned Italian plum tomatoes
3 teaspoons whole mixed pickling spice tied in cheesecloth
1 teaspoon Worcestershire sauce
¼ teaspoon Tabasco
2 quarts veal stock
10 tablespoons butter
10 tablespoons flour
¾ pound Vermont cheddar, double aged (4 years), shredded
1 cup butter
1 cup heavy cream
Salt and pepper to taste

Finely chop onions, celery, and carrots, sauté in olive oil in a 1-gallon soup pot until slightly softened. Add tomatoes, bag of spices, Worcestershire, and Tabasco; simmer 1 hour, stirring often.

Remove spice bag, reserve. Puree tomato mixture until smooth, return to rinsed pan; add veal stock and spice bag. Bring to boil, reduce heat, and simmer until reduced ¼.

Melt 10 tablespoons butter in a small pan, stir in flour to make a roux, cooking on low heat for about 5 minutes (do not brown). Whip the roux into the soup and bring to boil, simmering 10 minutes.

Add cheddar cheese, remaining butter, and cream; salt and pepper to taste. Serve immediately. If desired, the soup may be garnished with croutons, additional cheddar cheese, or chopped parsley.

ROAST CHRISTMAS GOOSE WITH ORANGE GRAVY
Serves 6 to 8

1 12- to 14-pound goose, dressed
2 pounds (2 large) onions, quartered
2 oranges, quartered
2 lemons, quartered
2 McIntosh apples, quartered
3 bay leaves
Salt and pepper
White wine, for deglazing

Clean goose thoroughly washing inside cavity; remove all cavity fat. Trim wing tips and drumstick knuckles, reserving with the neck, liver, heart, and giblets for stock. Singe bird if necessary.

Preheat oven to 350°.

Season cavity with salt and pepper. Stuff with onions, oranges, lemons, apples, and bay leaves. Truss or skewer to hold the legs together. Prick well around legs and back to allow fat to drain. Rub well with salt and pepper.

Roast approximately 20 minutes per pound, draining fat as it accumulates. When goose is done (180° internal), drain fat and deglaze pan with white wine, adding to goose stock for gravy.

GOOSE STOCK
Yield, 2 quarts

Reserved trimmings and giblets
½ pound onion, rough cut
¼ pound celery, rough cut
¼ pound carrots, rough cut
Parsley stems
2 bay leaves
6 whole black peppercorns
2 quarts water
½ cup white wine

Combine all ingredients and simmer 1½ to 2 hours. Add water as necessary to increase yield lost to reduction. Degrease.

GOOSE DEMI-GLAZE
Yield, 5 cups

½ pound onion, rough cut
¼ pound celery, rough cut
¼ pound carrots, rough cut
Drippings and enough fat to make 1 cup
1 cup flour
2 quarts Goose Stock
3 bay leaves
2 teaspoons tomato paste
Parsley stems
White wine, for deglazing
Salt and pepper

Caramelize vegetables in drippings. Add flour, cook together 10 minutes to make a roux. Add goose stock, bay leaves, tomato paste, and parsley. Simmer 1½ hours.

Remove vegetables and bay leaves; deglaze pan with white wine, season lightly with salt and pepper. Continue cooking until reduced to 5 cups.

Orange Gravy
Yield, about 2½ cups

5 tablespoons sugar
5 tablespoons red wine vinegar
2 oranges, sliced
1 lemon, sliced
¾ cup orange juice
5 cups Goose Demi-Glaze
2 tablespoons red currant jelly
5 tablespoons Cointreau
Salt and pepper

Slowly caramelize sugar in a saucepan over low heat. Add vinegar, orange and lemon slices, and orange juice, reduce by ½. Combine with demi-glaze and simmer 10 minutes. Add jelly and Cointreau. Simmer 5 minutes and season with salt and pepper.

❧

Apple-Apricot Chestnut Dressing
Serves 8 to 10

1 cup butter, or goose drippings
1 cup onions, diced
½ cup celery, diced
2 cups McIntosh apples, diced
6 cups crustless bread, diced
1½ cups apricots, diced
1 cup chestnuts, peeled, boiled, chopped
¼ cup parsley, chopped
2 teaspoons salt
1 teaspoon paprika
¼ cup Goose Stock

Preheat oven to 350º.
Melt ½ of the butter or drippings in a large pan. Sauté onions and celery until just tender, add apples and sauté 2 minutes. Add bread cubes and balance of ingredients. Mix until moist, but not wet.
Put in a buttered casserole and bake for 1 hour, moisten with additional stock if required.

❧

Baked Stuffed Potato Red Lion
Serves 8

8 baking potatoes, washed
4 teaspoons oil
8 tablespoons hot milk
5 tablespoons butter
2 tablespoons sour cream
1¼ teaspoons salt
¼ teaspoon pepper
3 tablespoons dried chives
¼ cup Parmesan cheese
¼ cup bacon bits
Paprika
6 tablespoons butter, melted

Preheat oven to 350º.
Rub potatoes with oil and prick twice with fork, bake for 1 hour.
Cut top off of each potato while still very hot. Scoop out potato and whip with milk, butter, sour cream, salt, pepper, and chives. Pipe filling back into the shells using a star tip. Sprinkle with Parmesan cheese and bacon bits, lightly dust with paprika, and drizzle with 1 tablespoon butter. Return to oven for 10 minutes until golden crisp.

❧

Vegetable Bundles
Serves 8

16 fresh medium asparagus spears
16 carrots, 2½ x ¼-inch julienne
16 red peppers, 2½ x ¼-inch julienne
8 green leek strips, 6 x ¼-inch, blanched
Salt and pepper
8 teaspoons melted butter
4 teaspoons white wine

Trim asparagus to 2½-inches long and remove any woody spots. Steam the asparagus, carrots, and peppers until tender. Blanch leek strips and chill immediately in cold water.
Preheat oven to 350º.
Place vegetables in bundles, tying with leek strips fashioned into bows.
Place bundles in a casserole and top each bundle with a sprinkle of salt, pepper, and 1 teaspoon butter. Add wine and heat to warm for 10 to 12 minutes.

❧

Red Lion Inn Chocolate Chip Pie
Yield, 1 9-inch pie

2⅔ cups all-purpose flour
2½ teaspoons baking powder
½ teaspoon salt
1 pound light brown sugar
1 teaspoon vanilla extract
12 tablespoons butter
3 eggs
1 small package chocolate chips
1 cup nuts, chopped
Melted butter

Preheat oven to 350º.
Blend together flour, baking powder, salt, sugar, vanilla, butter, and eggs. Mix in chocolate chips and nuts. Bake in a 9-inch pie pan for 35 minutes. After baking, drizzle top with melted butter. ❧

*H*APPY *N*EW *Y*EAR*!*

The Westin St. Francis
San Francisco, California

*S*ince opening its doors on March 21, 1904, The St. Francis has maintained its preeminence as San Francisco's center for social, theatrical, and business life for nearly nine decades. The city's landmark for celebration, with its ideal location on Union Square, the St. Francis has played host to thousands of New Year's Eve merrymakers through the years. The great Magneta clock in the lobby has been the traditional rendezvous, making "Meet me at the St. Francis" a New Year's resolution.

The St. Francis traditionally entertains guests observing the New Year with a scrumptious feast, wonderful music, and of course, luxurious surroundings. Here, Executive Chef Vlastimil Lebeda presents a New Year's feast for six, applying a California-style cooking approach to the freshest of winter ingredients.

Fillet of Rainbow Trout
with Caviar Beurre Blanc

Medley of Tender Leaves
with Winter Pear and Chopped Walnuts,
Creamy Lemon Sherry Dressing

Marinated Rack of Lamb
with Saffron Couscous
and Minted Cranberry-Orange Relish

Chocolate Crème Brûlée

COLOR PLATE 36

FILLET OF RAINBOW TROUT
Serves 6

6 3-ounce rainbow trout fillets, deboned, skin on
Salt and white pepper
⅓ cup butter

Season trout fillets with salt and pepper. Place in a preheated sauté pan with butter, sauté on both sides until done. Arrange fillets on serving dish, serve with Caviar Beurre Blanc.

CAVIAR BEURRE BLANC
6 Servings

1¼ cups fish stock
1¼ cups dry white wine
1 tablespoon shallots, chopped
¼ teaspoon fresh tarragon
½ cup cream
½ cup unsalted butter, cut in small cubes
¼ teaspoon lemon juice
Salt and pepper
½ ounce American sturgeon caviar

Combine fish stock, white wine, shallots, and tarragon in a pan, bring to a boil, reduce by ½; add cream, reduce to approximately ⅓ of total liquid.

Remove from heat. Whisk butter cubes into the sauce, 1 at a time; season with lemon juice, salt and pepper to taste. Strain sauce through cheesecloth or a fine sieve and keep hot, but do not allow to boil. Fold caviar into the sauce just before serving.

❧

MEDLEY OF TENDER LEAVES
WITH WINTER PEAR AND CHOPPED WALNUTS
Serves 6

1 small bunch watercress
1 head each: baby lettuce, red oak, green oak,
  limestone, frisée
3 pieces Belgian endive
1 pear, peeled, julienne
2 tablespoons walnuts, chopped

Clean and wash all greens, trim into smaller pieces. Arrange attractively on plates, top with julienne of pear and chopped walnuts. Serve with Lemon Sherry Dressing.

LEMON SHERRY DRESSING
Yield, approximately 2 cups

1 whole egg
¼ tablespoon shallots, chopped
1¼ cups salad oil
1 tablespoon red wine vinegar
1 tablespoon sherry
1 tablespoon dry vermouth
3 tablespoons fresh lemon juice
Salt and white pepper

Break egg into mixing bowl and whisk until slightly foamy; mix in shallots. While whisking constantly, slowly add oil until all is incorporated and fully emulsified. Gradually add vinegar, sherry, vermouth, and lemon juice. Adjust to taste with salt and pepper. Keep refrigerated if not serving until the next day.

❧

MARINATED RACK OF LAMB
Serves 5

¼ cup olive oil
1 teaspoon garlic, chopped
1 teaspoon fresh thyme, chopped
1 teaspoon rosemary, chopped
1 teaspoon black pepper, crushed
2 8-rib lamb racks, trimmed (all fat cover trimmed, the
  bones Frenched, leaving 2 inches of the bones
  exposed)
Salt

Mix olive oil and herbs in a bowl, brush the mixture over the lamb racks and refrigerate overnight.

Preheat oven to 400°.

Season the lamb with salt, arrange in a roasting pan and roast for 30 to 40 minutes, or until a meat thermometer registers 130° to 135° for medium-rare. Remove lamb from oven, keep warm. Allow it to rest approximately 10 minutes before serving. Cut racks into chops and serve with Saffron Couscous and Minted Cranberry-Orange Relish.

SAFFRON COUSCOUS
Serves 6

⅓ cup onion, chopped
1 tablespoon unsalted butter
1½ cups chicken stock, or water
Pinch saffron
1 cup couscous
Salt
1 tablespoon parsley, chopped

Cook the onion in the butter over moderately low heat for 1 minute; do not allow to brown. Add chicken stock or water, and saffron. Bring the liquid to a boil, stir in the couscous, season with salt and let the mixture stand, covered, off the heat for 5 minutes or until the couscous has absorbed the liquid. Mix in the chopped parsley and serve.

MINTED CRANBERRY-ORANGE RELISH
Yield, 1 cup

¼ cup water
¼ cup orange juice
½ cup sugar
½ pound fresh whole cranberries
1 tablespoon orange zest
¼ teaspoon dry English mustard
½ tablespoon fresh mint, chopped

Stir water, orange juice, and sugar in a saucepan until the sugar is thoroughly dissolved. Add the cranberries, bring to a boil, and cook for 3 to 5 minutes, stirring occasionally, until the skins of the berries are tender, but not mushy. Do not overcook.

Remove the pan from the heat and stir in the orange zest, dry mustard, and chopped mint. Transfer the mixture to a bowl and let cool, then chill for 1 to 2 hours before serving. The relish may be prepared a day in advance.

CHOCOLATE CRÈME BRÛLÉE
Yield, 12 servings

1 quart heavy cream
½ vanilla bean, or 1 tablespoon vanilla extract
15 egg yolks
¼ cup sugar
5 ounces semisweet chocolate, grated,
  or chocolate morsels
Turbinado sugar (raw sugar), or brown sugar
Fresh raspberries

Heat cream with vanilla to simmering. Whip together egg yolks and sugar. Gradually add hot cream to the eggs, stir, remove vanilla bean.

Place crème brûlée mixture over a saucepan with water; set to medium heat. Stir occasionally with a spoon, being careful not to let the water boil. Cook until the mixture coats the back of a spoon. Remove from heat.

Place chocolate in the bottom of a low 8-inch ceramic dish or 12 individual custard cups. Divide the custard mixture evenly into the cups over the chocolate, refrigerate.

At serving time, sprinkle each with raw or brown sugar and set under broiler until the sugar caramelizes. Serve with fresh raspberries.

SUPPLEMENTAL RECIPES & TECHNIQUES

POPOVERS
THE SAGAMORE
Yield, 12 popovers

5 whole eggs, beaten
2 cups milk
1 cup all-purpose flour
Salt and nutmeg to taste
Vegetable shortening

Preheat oven to 350°.

Blend eggs with milk, mix well. Add flour, salt, and nutmeg to taste, and whip into a smooth batter.

Generously grease muffin pans with shortening. Place greased pans in the oven for 8 to 10 minutes, until pans are quite hot. Carefully remove pans from oven and pour in the batter, filling cups ⅔ full. Return the pans to the oven and bake for 25 minutes, until golden brown. Serve hot with butter.

CREOLE SEASONING
LAFAYETTE HOTEL
Yield, approximately ⅓ cup

¼ cup salt
1 tablespoon granulated garlic
1 tablespoon black pepper
1 tablespoon paprika
¾ teaspoon onion powder
¼ teaspoon cayenne pepper
¼ teaspoon dried oregano
¼ teaspoon dried thyme

Mix ingredients, store in a tightly sealed container. Good on roasted or grilled seafood, meat, and poultry.

TOMATO BUTTER SAUCE
LAFAYETTE HOTEL
Serves 6

⅔ cup dry white wine
⅓ cup white wine vinegar
¼ cup shallots, minced
1½ pounds beefsteak tomatoes, peeled, seeded, diced, well drained
2 tablespoons heavy cream
1½ cups butter, chilled, cut by tablespoons
4 teaspoons lemon juice
Salt and white pepper

Bring wine, vinegar, and shallots to boil until reduced, about 5 minutes. Add ½ the tomatoes, add cream, return to boil. Reduce heat to low and whisk in butter, 1 piece at a time. Remove pan from heat briefly if beads of butter appear. Add remaining tomatoes and the lemon juice. Salt and pepper to taste. Remove from heat, keep warm.

WHITE CHOCOLATE BROWNIES
LAFAYETTE HOTEL
Yield, 1 8-inch square pan

Butter, for pan
7 tablespoons unsalted butter
8 ounces white chocolate, finely chopped
2 eggs at room temperature
Pinch salt
½ cup sugar
1 cup all-purpose flour
1½ teaspoons vanilla extract
4 ounces bittersweet or semi-sweet chocolate, finely chopped
Dark Chocolate Sauce
Vanilla Bean Ice Cream

Preheat oven to 350°.

Lightly butter an 8-inch baking pan, line with foil, butter foil.

Melt butter over low heat. Remove from heat and add ½ the white chocolate; do not stir. Using electric mixer, blend eggs and salt. Gradually add sugar and beat until pale yellow and ribbon forms when beaters are lifted. Add butter mixture, flour, and vanilla, beat just until smooth. Mix in dark chocolate and remaining white chocolate. Spread batter in pan, bake until edges are brown and top begins to color and crack, about 30 minutes. Cool on rack 4 hours.

Cut brownies into 2-inch squares. Place 1 on each plate. Spoon Dark Chocolate Sauce around brownie, and drizzle some over. Serve Vanilla Bean Ice Cream aside.

DARK CHOCOLATE SAUCE
LAFAYETTE HOTEL
Yield, 1½ cups

½ cup heavy cream
3 tablespoons unsalted butter, cut into pieces
⅓ cup sugar
⅓ cup dark brown sugar, firmly packed
½ cup unsweetened cocoa, sifted
Pinch salt
½ cup strong coffee

Bring cream and butter to boil over medium heat, stirring until butter melts. Add both sugars and mix until dissolved. Reduce heat to low. Add cocoa and salt, whisk until smooth. Remove from heat and stir in the coffee. Serve warm or at room temperature. May be refrigerated up to 3 days.

VANILLA BEAN ICE CREAM
LAFAYETTE HOTEL
Yield, about 2 quarts

2½ cups milk
3½ cups heavy cream
1 vanilla bean, split lengthwise
2 cups sugar
12 egg yolks

Scald milk and 1½ cups cream with vanilla bean, remove from heat. Scrape vanilla beans from pod into mixture, return bean, steep 10 minutes.

Add 1 cup sugar to mixture and stir until dissolved. Bring to boil, stirring constantly. Beat yolks and remaining sugar until pale yellow and a ribbon forms when beaters are lifted. Gradually add the hot milk mixture, stirring. Return to saucepan and stir over low heat until custard thickens and coats spoon, do not boil. Strain into a bowl, mix in remaining cream.

Set bowl over larger bowl of ice water to let custard chill, stir occasionally. Transfer custard to ice cream maker, process according to manufacturer's instructions. Freeze several hours, covered, to meld flavors.

SLY BREAD
EL ENCANTO
Yield, 1 2-pound loaf

One:
1½ cups bread flour*
1½ cups warm water
½ tablespoon sugar
1 tablespoon dry yeast
Two:
2¼ cups bread flour*
1 tablespoon kosher salt

One: mix a "sponge" of flour, water, sugar, and yeast in a large bowl. Let rise 30 minutes to 1 hour at room temperature.

Two: mix flour and salt. Place "sponge" in a bowl with dough hook, add flour/salt mixture; mix/knead for 6 minutes on low in a food processor or blender, and for 8 minutes on high, or 15 minutes by hand. Cover with plastic wrap, let rise until doubled.

Form into a single loaf, allow to rise again until doubled.

Preheat oven to 350°.

Bake for 40 minutes or until done, spraying heavily with water from a spray bottle several times during baking.

*General Mills "Better for Bread" is good for home use.

TRUFFLED CABBAGE RAVIOLI
EL ENCANTO
Yield, 32 ravioli

7 cups cabbage, deveined, ¼-inch diced
Salted water
4 tablespoons unsalted butter
1 tablespoon shallots, finely diced
Salt and freshly ground black pepper
3 tablespoons canned truffle juice
4 tablespoons black truffles*, fresh or frozen, finely chopped
1 tablespoon cognac
1 recipe Provençal Ravioli Dough
Flour and cornmeal, for dusting
* Any fresh or dried mushrooms may be substituted.

Blanch cabbage in heavily salted water for 1 minute, refresh in cold water, drain. Melt the butter in a sauté pan, add the shallots and sauté until clear. Add the cabbage, season with salt and pepper. Add the truffle juice and truffles, and cognac. Continue cooking over low heat until liquid is reduced and mixture dries. The cabbage should be tender but firm. Remove to a plate to cool.

Stuff ravioli in 1 x 1-inch squares and place on parchment paper dusted with cornmeal to prevent sticking. (Ravioli may be refrigerated or frozen for several days.)

To cook, carefully drop ravioli into a large pot of boiling salted water. They will soon float to the top when done. Remove from water with a skimmer, drain. Serve with melted butter or venison au jus.

PROVENÇAL RAVIOLI DOUGH
EL ENCANTO
Yield, dough for 32 ravioli

1½ cups all-purpose flour
4 tablespoons unsalted butter, room temperature
½ cup (or less) cool water
1 tablespoon salt

Mix flour, butter, salt, and water until a smooth dough forms. Knead slowly until the dough is firm yet supple. Store covered until ready to use.

Ravioli, to make:

Split dough evenly, roll out each of the 2 portions on work surface to 1/16-inch thick, or use a pasta machine to roll to desired thickness.

If using a ravioli pan: fit pan with 1 sheet of dough. Stuff each pocket with filling, pressing to remove air under the dough. Cover with another sheet of prepared dough, use a rolling pin to seal ravioli and trim excess dough.

To create by hand: set 1 sheet of dough on a work surface. Place 1 teaspoon filling at 1- to 2-inch intervals along the sheet. Top with another sheet of dough. Press down around each pocket of filling to remove air and seal. Cut into squares.

Floating Islands
El Encanto
Serves 8

1 cup egg whites
Pinch salt
2 teaspoons lemon juice or cream of tartar
2 cups sugar
½ cup almonds, slivered, toasted
Crème Anglaise

Ingredients should be at room temperature.

Place egg whites in a mixing bowl, add salt and lemon juice. Mix first at low speed, gradually increasing speed. When soft peaks form, gradually add 1 cup sugar. Do not overbeat, as eggs will be dry and crumbly.

Shape egg whites with large cooking spoon and drop into a wide pan of simmering water. Cover and simmer 7 to 10 minutes, until done (turn off the heat and allow to sit in the water several minutes to continue cooking). Remove, drain, and cool on a towel.

Top meringues with toasted almonds. Caramelize 1 cup sugar by cooking until it liquifies and turns golden, drizzle over the meringue "islands." To serve, float atop Crème Anglaise in a bowl.

Crème Anglaise
El Encanto
Yield, 5 cups

1 pint whole milk
1 vanilla bean, split lengthwise
12 egg yolks
6 tablespoons sugar
Pinch salt
1 cup heavy cream

In a thick-bottomed nonreactive pan (like stainless steel), heat milk over low heat with the vanilla bean. In a large bowl, whisk egg yolks immediately with the sugar and salt until they are a pale yellow and form a thick ribbon when lifted with the whisk.

Temper eggs by quickly whisking in a small amount of the heated milk. Pour the mixture into the hot milk, whisking constantly over low heat until the mixture slightly thickens. Do not overcook. When thick enough to coat spoon without running, remove from heat and strain into a bowl set in ice. Add the cream, chill until used.

Pear Pecan Barley
The American Club
Serves 10

4 tablespoons butter
1 onion, finely diced
2 cloves garlic, chopped
1 bay leaf
5 sprigs fresh thyme, chopped
Chicken stock
Salt and pepper
1 pound pearl barley
½ cup pecans, chopped
2 pears, finely diced
2 tablespoons pear brandy

Melt 2 tablespoons butter in a saucepot, sauté onions until translucent, add garlic, bay leaf, and thyme. Add sufficient chicken stock to cover barley for cooking, season with salt and pepper. Add barley and simmer gently until the barley is tender.

Melt remaining butter and carefully sauté the chopped pecans to toast them, but do not brown. Add the diced pears and sauté until warmed.

Flame the pears and pecans with the brandy, stir into the cooked barley, serve.

Root Vegetable Julienne
The American Club
Serves 12 to 14

1 pound carrots, peeled, julienne
1 pound turnips, peeled, julienne
1 pound rutabagas, peeled, julienne
1 bunch leeks, washed well, julienne
Salt and pepper

Blanch the vegetables in boiling salted water until al dente (about 10 seconds) and drain.

Place vegetables in a warmed bowl and toss with thin slices of Herbed Butter until it melts.

Season to taste, serve.

Herbed Butter
The American Club
Yield, 1 pound

1 pound butter
6 shallots, peeled, finely diced
2 cloves garlic, peeled, finely chopped
3 sprigs fresh basil, finely chopped
6 sprigs fresh thyme, stemmed, chopped
1 bunch chives, chopped
Juice of 1 lemon
Salt and pepper

Place all ingredients in a food processor and blend until smooth.

Spoon the butter onto parchment paper and roll into a 1-inch tube, twist ends, refrigerate.

BOURBON CARAMEL APPLE GRATIN
THE AMERICAN CLUB
Serves 4

Pastry cream:
2 cups milk
4 whole eggs
1 cup granulated sugar
½ cup cornstarch
½ cup butter, softened
1½ cups heavy cream
Bourbon to taste

Heat milk to boiling. Meanwhile, beat eggs and sugar together to ribbon stage, add cornstarch just to blend. Add some of the hot milk to the egg mixture to temper, add all back at once to the hot milk, return to boil while whisking continuously. Whisk while boiling 1 minute.

Remove from heat, whisk in butter until incorporated. Chill. When cold, whip the pastry cream until smooth, add the heavy cream until a thick pouring cream is achieved. Flavor to taste with bourbon.

Caramelized apples:
1 cup sugar
6 large tart apples, peeled, cored, sliced
1 tablespoon superfine sugar
Sprig of mint

Place sugar in a wide pan over medium high heat, stir constantly until sugar liquifies and turns a rich mahogany color. Do not allow to smoke. When the sugar begins to turn color, add the apples. The apples will cook quickly and be covered with the caramel. Cook until the apples are soft and tender.

Place 1 serving of the apples on dessert dish. Reserve 3 nice slices per plate for garnish. Pour some of the pastry cream over each until the apples are covered. Sprinkle each with the superfine sugar. Place under broiler until the sugar is caramelized and sauce begins to bubble. Garnish side of plate with fanned apple slices and sprig of mint.

RASPBERRY AND FRESH THYME SORBET
THE GREENBRIER
Yield, 1 pint

1½ cups raspberry puree (1½ pounds raspberries), strained
½ cup sugar
4 tablespoons honey
2 tablespoons lemon juice
3 tablespoons Chambord
½ tablespoon fresh thyme leaves

Mix all ingredients together, except thyme. Run through an ice cream freezer. Fold in the thyme when the sorbet has finished churning.

LEMON CURD
THE GREENBRIER
Yield, about 2 cups

1 cup butter
1¼ cups sugar
Juice and zest of 4 lemons
4 eggs

Combine the butter and sugar in a saucepan, heat. In a mixing bowl, beat eggs, then add lemon juice. Strain, add to the heated butter along with the lemon zest. Cook over medium heat until it reaches a sauce consistency.

ALMOND TUILES
STOUFFER MAYFLOWER HOTEL
Yield, 18 tuiles

1 cup sugar
1 cup butter
¾ cup all-purpose flour
¾ cup almonds, finely chopped
Pinch salt
⅓ cup heavy cream

Preheat oven to 400°.
Mix sugar and butter until moist. Add flour, almonds, pinch of salt, cream, and mix. Roll into 18 ½-ounce balls. Place balls on cookie sheet and bake for 8 minutes or until light brown and in uniform circles.

ACORN SQUASH WITH HONEY
THE HOMESTEAD
Serves 4

For each squash half:
1 teaspoon butter
1 teaspoon honey
Pinch ground ginger
Pinch ground cinnamon
Pinch salt

Preheat oven to 325°.
Slice squash in half evenly from stem end to blossom end; trim a slice from the bottom of each half so they will sit evenly. Scoop out seeds and stringy material, set squash in baking pan; put butter, honey, ginger, cinnamon, and salt into each cavity.

Bake for 40 to 50 minutes until very soft. Serve hot.

Sweet Potatoes Duchesse

The Homestead

Serves 6

2 pounds sweet potatoes, washed and dried
4 tablespoons butter
2 tablespoons sugar
Pinch salt
Pinch ground ginger
Pinch cinnamon
2 egg yolks
2 tablespoons heavy cream
Butter for baking sheet

Preheat oven to 350°.

Bake potatoes until soft, 45 to 55 minutes. When cool enough to handle, cut potatoes in half, scoop out pulp, discard skins. Puree pulp with butter until smooth. Place puree in a sauté pan over medium heat; season with sugar, salt, ginger, and cinnamon. Cook until bubbling, stirring often. Reduce heat to low. Whisk together egg yolks and cream, stir the mixture into the potatoes. Let cool.

Butter a baking sheet and pipe the potatoes onto the sheet with a star tip, making circles for individual servings. Bake 10 minutes or until lightly browned.

Double Applesauce Cake

The Homestead

Yield, 1 10-inch cake

8 tablespoons butter
1 cup sugar
1 teaspoon vanilla extract
1 egg
2 cups plus 2 tablespoons all-purpose flour
¾ teaspoon baking soda
¼ teaspoon allspice
½ teaspoon cinnamon
¼ teaspoon nutmeg, freshly ground
1⅓ cups raisins
1 cup walnuts, chopped
¾ cup crushed pineapple, drained
½ cup candied cherries, chopped
1 cup applesauce
Butter and flour for pan

Preheat oven to 350°.

Use an electric mixer to cream the butter until fluffy; add the sugar gradually until dissolved. Scraping the sides of the bowl often, add vanilla, blend well, then add the egg, and mix at medium speed until fully combined. Sift the flour with the baking soda, allspice, cinnamon, and nutmeg; stir mixture into the batter. Add the raisins, walnuts, pineapple, cherries, and applesauce, stir until blended. Pour into a buttered and floured 10-inch pan. Bake for about 45 minutes or until the cake pulls slightly away from the sides of the pan and a tester comes out clean when put in the center of the cake.

Turn cake out on a rack to cool.

Cracked Wheat Bread

Omni Netherland Plaza

Yield, 2 loaves

2 cups cracked wheat
1 cup brown sugar
1 tablespoon salt
2 tablespoons butter
2 cups boiling water
2 tablespoons plus 1 teaspoon dry yeast
8 cups bread flour
1 cup tepid water

Put the cracked wheat, brown sugar, salt, and butter in a large stainless steel bowl; pour the boiling water over the mixture and stir to melt the butter; let the mixture cool to 90° to 110°.

Put the yeast in the mixer bowl with dough hook; add 3 cups tepid water; let stand 10 to 15 minutes; pour cooled cracked wheat mixture into mixer bowl. Add bread flour, turn mixer on low, and mix until flour is combined with liquid; add enough extra flour to make a dough that is light, but not sticky. Mix on dough hook for 20 minutes.

Turn out dough into an oiled bowl, cover with a damp cloth and let rise until doubled in bulk.

Punch down, cut into either 1-pound loaves, or 1-ounce rolls; let rise. Preheat oven to 350° and bake until done (50 to 60 minutes for loaves, 20 to 30 minutes for rolls); brush tops with melted butter.

Pear Butter

Omni Netherland Plaza

Yield, 4 cups

2 cups pear pulp
1 cup sugar
½ teaspoon orange zest
3 tablespoons fresh orange juice
¼ teaspoon ground nutmeg

Quarter and core the pears; cook until soft, adding only enough water to prevent sticking. Put through a food mill. Add remaining ingredients; simmer until thickened, about 15 minutes. Put in a container, cover and refrigerate.

MISSISSIPPI MUD PIE
THE DELTA QUEEN
Serves 6

Chocolate Pecan Brownie:
4 ounces unsweetened chocolate
½ pound unsalted butter, softened
2 cups sugar
½ teaspoon salt
4 eggs
1 teaspoon vanilla extract
1 cup flour
1 cup pecan pieces

Preheat oven to 375°.

Melt chocolate and let cool. Whip butter and add sugar, salt, eggs, and vanilla, mix well. Add melted chocolate and flour and mix well. Fold in the pecans. Pour into a greased 8 x 11 x 2-inch greased pan and bake for approximately 30 minutes. Turn out on a flat surface and cool.

Coffee Ice Cream:
2 cups whole milk
3 cups heavy cream
1¼ cups sugar
4 eggs
½ teaspoon vanilla extract
¼ cup coffee reduction (4 cups coffee reduced to ¼ cup)

Scald milk and cream. Add sugar and dissolve. In a separate bowl, beat eggs, vanilla, and coffee reduction. Slowly add milk mixture to eggs, whipping continuously. Return to heat and cook over low heat, stirring constantly, until mixture coats a spoon, about 15 minutes. Refrigerate overnight and freeze in an ice cream freezer.

Chocolate Whipped Cream:
2 cups heavy cream
1 cup confectioners' sugar
2 teaspoons chocolate liqueur

Whip ingredients together in a chilled mixing bowl until stiff.

To serve:
Chocolate Pecan Brownie
Coffee Ice Cream
Chocolate Whipped Cream
Chocolate syrup, warmed
Pecan pieces, for garnish

Top brownie with ice cream and freeze until set. Top with whipped cream and freeze. Cut into 6 to 8 equal portions and top with warmed chocolate syrup. Garnish with pecan pieces.

KAHLÚA CRÊPES
THE DELTA QUEEN
Serves 6

Crêpes:
2 eggs
⅔ cup milk
2 tablespoons and 2 teaspoons butter, melted
⅓ cup all-purpose flour
Pinch salt
Vegetable oil, as needed
Strawberries, for garnish

Mix eggs, milk, butter, flour, and salt in a blender or food processor for 30 seconds and scrape down bowl. Mix until very smooth. Adjust consistency to that of heavy cream with additional flour or water. Let rest 30 minutes.

Heat crêpe pan over medium-high heat. For each crêpe, brush pan with oil, pour about 3 tablespoons mix in center of pan and tilt until bottom is covered. Cook until edges are brown and underside is golden, flip and cook 1 minute. Remove to serving plate.

Fill center of crêpe with whipped filling and fold over to create a half moon. Use a pastry bag to border crêpe with additional filling, garnish with a strawberry. Top with ¼ cup Kahlúa Sauce.

Whipped filling:
2 cups heavy cream
⅓ cup confectioners' sugar
2 teaspoons Kahlúa

Whip together in a chilled bowl until stiff.

Kahlúa Sauce:
1 cup butter
1 ounce semisweet chocolate
1 cup light brown sugar, packed
½ cup Kahlúa
¼ cup heavy cream

Melt butter and chocolate over low heat, add sugar and dissolve, stirring until smooth. Add Kahlúa and mix well. Stir in cream and remove from heat. Serve warm.

HERSHEY CHARLOTTE
THE HOTEL HERSHEY
Yield, 12 3¼-ounce charlotte molds

1 cup plus ⅛ cup milk
½ cup sugar
2 tablespoons cornstarch
¼ cup milk, cold
6 egg yolks
1 teaspoon powdered gelatin mixed with
  2 tablespoons cold water
⅓ cup raspberry puree, seeds strained
¼ cup Hershey's American Cocoa
2 cups heavy cream

Bring 1 cup plus ⅛ cup milk and sugar to a boil. Dissolve cornstarch in ¼ cup cold milk, add egg yolks. Temper egg mixture with a bit of the hot milk, combine both and bring to a boil, add gelatin/water mix, remove from heat.

Put about ⅓ of the above base into a separate bowl and add raspberry puree, let cool.

Add Hershey's American Cocoa to the bowl containing ⅔ the base mixture, whisk until dissolved and smooth.

When both bases are completely cool, whip 1⅓ cups cream into soft peaks and fold into the chocolate base. Whip ⅔ cup cream to soft peaks and fold into the raspberry base.

Fill a pastry bag with #8 plain tip with chocolate cream, fill each mold ⅔ full. Fill another pastry bag with #5 plain tip with raspberry cream. Put tip into the center of the chocolate cream and squeeze out enough raspberry cream so molds fill. Level molds with a palate knife to flatten, refrigerate overnight. To unmold, set each mold in a pan of warm water for 15 to 20 seconds, turn mold upside down and shake or tap to release the charlotte.

Serve with English Apricot Sauce and Amaretti Cookies.

ENGLISH APRICOT SAUCE
THE HOTEL HERSHEY
Yield, Variable

English Apricot Sauce is a combination of Apricot Sauce and Sauce Anglaise. The Hotel Hershey uses 3 parts Apricot Sauce to 1 part Sauce Anglaise, but it may be adjusted to your personal taste.

APRICOT SAUCE
THE HOTEL HERSHEY
Yield, 2 cups

1 cup apricot marmalade
1 cup canned apricots, drained

Puree marmalade smooth, add enough water to create a sauce of medium consistency. Puree canned apricots until smooth and add to the marmalade puree. Strain and adjust consistency, if necessary.

SAUCE ANGLAISE
THE HOTEL HERSHEY
Yield, approximately 1½ cups

1 cup milk
4 tablespoons sugar
¾ teaspoon vanilla extract
3 egg yolks, beaten
1 tablespoon Cointreau

Bring milk, sugar, and vanilla to a boil. Beat egg yolks, temper with some of the heated milk, combine the mixtures and cook gently while stirring until the mixture starts to thicken. Do not overheat as the mixture will separate. Remove from heat and stir in Cointreau.

AMARETTI COOKIES
THE HOTEL HERSHEY
Yield, approximately 2 dozen quarter-sized cookies

⅓ cup almonds, very finely ground
¾ cup sugar
3 tablespoons egg whites
Confectioners' sugar

Blend ground almonds, sugar, and egg whites in a mixer, using a paddle, for 1 to 2 minutes. Fill a pastry bag with #5 plain tip and pipe out round cookies on a cookie sheet. Dust liberally with confectioners' sugar. Allow to rest at room temperature overnight.

Preheat oven to 350°.

Bake approximately 10 minutes until cookies begin to brown on the edges, cool.

BASIC BROWN SAUCE
Yield, about 2 cups

1 clove garlic, minced
1 medium onion, chopped
1 carrot, chopped
¼ cup butter
¼ cup all-purpose flour
3 cups beef stock
½ cup tomato puree
½ teaspoon dried thyme
1 bay leaf
2 teaspoons dried parsley
Salt and pepper

Sauté garlic, onion, and carrot until lightly browned. Stir in flour, lower heat, and cook until it is golden, about 8 minutes; whisk often. Whisk in beef stock all at once, beat in tomato puree, add herbs. Cover partially, simmer gently until reduced by about ⅓, 45 minutes to 1 hour. Strain, season with salt and pepper.

❧

BOILED LOBSTER

For each lobster, heat 1½ quarts water with 1½ tablespoons salt to boiling. Plunge lobsters headfirst into the water, cover, reheat to boiling; reduce heat. Simmer 10 minutes, drain. Place lobster on its back, cut lengthwise with a sharp knife from head to tip of tail. Remove the stomach (just behind the head), and the intestinal vein which runs from the stomach to the end of the tail. Save the green liver (tomalley) and any coral-colored roe. Crack the claws to remove the claw meat.

❧

CLARIFIED BUTTER

Heat butter gently in a saucepan until melted; spoon off any foam. Remove from heat, allow it to sit until solids have settled. Reserve the clear yellow liquid from the top, discard the solids.

❧

CRÈME FRAÎCHE
Yield, about 2 cups

2 cups heavy cream
1 tablespoon cultured buttermilk

In a small saucepan, blend together cream and buttermilk. Heat over low heat, stirring gently, until a thermometer reads 85°. Remove from heat and pour the mixture into a just-scalded 1-quart jar. Cover loosely with waxed paper, set aside at room temperature for 8 to 24 hours until it reaches the consistency of whipped cream. Cover tightly, refrigerate.

CREOLE SAUCE
Yield, 2½ cups

½ cup green bell pepper, chopped
½ cup red bell pepper, chopped
1 cup onion, chopped
2 cups tomatoes, diced
½ teaspoon tarragon
½ teaspoon oregano
½ teaspoon sweet basil
½ teaspoon thyme
2 tablespoons butter
2 cloves garlic, thin sliced
½ teaspoon Old Bay seasoning
1 teaspoon Tabasco
5 bay leaves

In sauté pan, place peppers, onion, tomatoes, tarragon, oregano, basil, thyme, and butter, sauté for 2 to 3 minutes. Before the onion becomes transparent, add garlic, Old Bay, Tabasco, and bay leaves. Simmer the sauce to reduce by ⅓. Cool.

❧

MAYONNAISE
THE HOMESTEAD
Yield, 5 cups

The superior taste of your own "mayo" makes its creation well worth the effort. Mayonnaise's critical secrets: warm ingredients and extreme care taken in the initial bonding of the oil and egg yolks.

6 egg yolks at room temperature
½ teaspoon salt
Pinch freshly ground white pepper
Juice of one large or two small lemons
1 tablespoon vinegar (white, red wine, or cider)
1 teaspoon Dijon mustard
1 teaspoon dry English mustard
3 to 4 drops Worcestershire sauce
4 cups oil (3 of peanut oil, 1 of olive oil)
Pinch cayenne pepper (optional)

Warm a mixing bowl by filling with hot water, pouring it out and drying completely with a cloth towel. Add egg yolks and use an electric mixer to mix until thickened. Add all ingredients except oil, mix thoroughly until smooth and all dry mustard is dissolved.

Begin adding oil, in a very fine stream of droplets at first, until ½ cup has been added. Then add more quickly until all is incorporated. (Mayonnaise that is too thick may be thinned with a touch of hot water, lemon juice, or vinegar.)

Adjust seasoning, chill. Keeps well for a week to 10 days refrigerated in a glass jar.

HOLLANDAISE SAUCE
Yield, 1½ cups

3 egg yolks
1 tablespoon water
Salt and fresh-ground pepper
¾ cup butter, cut in small pieces, chilled
1½ tablespoons lemon juice

In a small saucepan, combine yolks, water, and a sprinkle of salt and pepper. Set in a hot (not boiling, or the eggs will curdle) water bath and whisk until mixture is smooth. Bit by bit, whisk in butter until incorporated, continue whisking until thick and creamy. Add lemon juice, adjust seasoning.

❧

SIMPLE SYRUP
Yield, 4 cups

In a large saucepan, combine 1 pound sugar and 1 quart water, heat to boiling. Cool.

❧

SHRIMP STOCK
LAFAYETTE HOTEL
Yield, 2 cups

3½ cups water
¼ cup dry white wine
6 ounces shrimp shells
½ medium leek, chopped
1 small celery stalk, chopped
½ small carrot, chopped
½ small onion, chopped
½ bay leaf

Combine all ingredients in a large saucepan and bring to a boil. Reduce heat and simmer 35 minutes. Strain stock, return to pot, and boil until reduced to 2 cups, if necessary.

❧

RABBIT STOCK
LAFAYETTE HOTEL
Yield, 12 cups

5½ quarts rich chicken stock
Reserved rabbit bones
2 onions, diced
2 leeks, sliced
3 bay leaves

Combine all ingredients in a stock pot. Bring to boil, reduce heat and simmer, occasionally skimming surface. Remove from heat after 1 hour and strain; degrease. Return to a clean stock pot and reduce to 12 cups.

BASIC STOCK
Yield, about 8 cups

1 4- to 5-pound stewing chicken;
   or 4 to 5 pounds beef or veal bones and trimmings*;
   or 2 to 3 pounds fish heads, bones and trimmings*, or shellfish and trimmings
Water to cover
3 whole carrots
1 or 2 large onions, whole
1 stalk celery, with leaves
1 leek, split and/or 1 whole bulb of garlic (optional)
1 bouquet garni
4 to 6 whole black peppercorns

*If you like, deeply oven-brown (do not burn) the bones and trimmings in a 450° oven for 45 minutes to 1 hour prior to boiling to add richness to the broth.

Place meat or fish in a large pot with water to cover by about 2 inches. Bring to a boil slowly, repeatedly skimming off scum as it appears. Add balance of ingredients, bring to another boil, then lower heat to lowest possible simmer.

Cooking time:

Chicken, 2 to 3 hours, depending on the age of the bird.

Meats, 4 to 5 hours.

Fish and shellfish, 35 to 45 minutes.

(A shorter cooking time is followed should you wish to serve any of the meats afterward, a longer time for a richer flavored broth.)

Strain the stock through a colander lined with cheesecloth. The stock may be diluted with water or further reduced to achieve desired concentration. The stock may be refrigerated for 3 to 4 days, or frozen for later use.

❧

COURT BOUILLON
Yield, about 2 quarts

2 quarts water
1 stalk celery
3 sprigs parsley
1 medium onion, halved
1 bay leaf
¾ cup cider vinegar
Head and bones of any white-meat fish
8 to 10 black peppercorns
Pinch thyme
¾ teaspoon salt

Combine all ingredients and simmer uncovered for 20 minutes. Strain through a fine mesh strainer or cheesecloth to obtain a clear liquid. Add water, if necessary, to make up for reduction losses.

POACHED EGGS

Water
2 to 3 tablespoons white vinegar
Salt (optional)
Eggs at room temperature

Put water to about 1-inch deep in a skillet, add vinegar and salt, bring to a boil, reduce heat to low. Break eggs, 1 at a time, into a saucer and gently slide into the water. Steep until done to desired firmness. Remove with a slotted spatula to drain.

❧

RASPBERRY PUREE

If using fresh berries, whir in a blender and strain to remove seeds.

If using frozen berries, you will need 2 10-ounce packages to make 2 cups of puree. Let them thaw completely, drain off the sugar syrup, then proceed as with fresh berries.

❧

BASIC PIE CRUST
Makes 2 9-inch pie shells

3 cups flour
2 cups shortening
1 cup water
Dash salt
1 teaspoon vinegar

Place flour and salt in bowl. Cut in shortening until it resembles the size of small peas. Add the water and vinegar and incorporate into dough, do not over mix. Divide dough in half, cover with waxed paper and refrigerate for 1 hour to allow dough to relax. Dust lightly with flour, roll to desired size and place in pie pans.

BOUQUET GARNI

3 to 4 sprigs of parsley, 1 sprig of thyme, and 1 bay leaf tied together in cheesecloth.

❧

GLACE DE VIANDE

Brown Sauce (page 117) reduced to syrup consistency.

❧

CARAMEL SAUCE
THE DON CESAR
Serves 8

1 cup sugar
2 tablespoons water
1 teaspoon lemon juice
½ cup whipping cream
1 tablespoon unsalted butter

Place sugar in a small saucepan, moisten with water and lemon juice. Melt sugar over medium heat, using a wooden spoon to keep sugar off the sides of the pan. When sugar turns nutty brown, remove from heat to avoid burning, add cream and butter (splattering will occur, use caution). Return pan to stove to warm mixture while mixing. Keep warm until ready to serve. ❧

GLOSSARY

Al Dente: cooked until tender yet firm to the bite

Amaretto: almond liqueur

Andouille: a highly seasoned Cajun smoked pork sausage

Au Jus: cooked meat's naturally rendered juices, usually defatted prior to serving

Blanch: to scald vegetables in boiling water for a few moments

Bouillon: stock or broth

Bouquet Garni: herbs tied in cheesecloth for easy addition and removal in soups or stews

Braise: to cook meat with a small amount of liquid in a covered pan or casserole

Brown: to briefly fry meat in a little fat or butter until browned on the outside

Caramelize: to turn sugars to a golden brown by cooking over low heat

Cassis: black currant brandy

Chambord: a raspberry liqueur

Chorizo: a spicy, dried sausage used in Spanish-influenced cooking

Clarified Butter: butter from which the milk solids have been removed

Cointreau: an orange-flavored liqueur

Coulis: a coarsely chopped vegetable sauce, including juices

Count: the number required to equal 1 pound

Court Bouillon: salted water or any more complex stock used for cooking fish

Crème de Cacao: chocolate liqueur

Croutons: small bread cubes baked, fried, or toasted until crisp

Deglaze: to use a liquid to remove the cooked-on food residues from a pan

Demi-Glace: stock reduced to a syrup consistency

Dredge: to fully immerse in a coating, usually flour, prior to cooking

Egg Wash: eggs beaten with or without an added liquid to be used as a glaze

Filé: powdered young leaves of sassafras, often used in thickening soups and stews

Finish: the last in a series of steps in cooking or plate preparation

Flame: to ignite for the purpose of burning off alcohol

Framboise: raspberry liqueur

Frangelico: a hazelnut liqueur, infused with berries and flowers

French: to strip the meat from the end of the bone (usually ribs) to expose the bone

Glace de Viande: brown stock that has been reduced to a syrup consistency

Grand Marnier: an orange liqueur

Grenadine: a pomegranate syrup

Heavy Cream: grade of cream containing the most fats, usually sold as "whipping" cream

Julienne: to cut into matchstick-sized pieces

Kahlúa: coffee liqueur

Kirschwasser (or Kirsch): a cherry brandy

Marinade: a liquid containing an acid and seasonings, used for tenderizing and flavoring

Marinate: to allow to soak for a period of time in a marinade

Nonreactive Pan: cooking utensils unaffected by acids such as stainless steel, glass, or porcelain

Parboil: to boil until partly cooked to match the cooking time of companion foods

Phyllo (or Filo) Dough: a many-layered puff pastry

Poach: to cook in just enough boiling liquid to cover

Puree: foods machine- or seive-processed to a smooth, thick consistency

Reduce: to boil to evaporate a liquid, reducing its volume

Roux: a cooked paste of equal amounts of flour and a fat used as a thickening agent

Sake: Japanese rice wine

Scallions: also known as green onions or spring onions

Score: to cut shallow slits at regular intervals

Sear: to cook meat quickly over high heat to seal in juices

Spring onions: green onions or scallions

Sweat: to intensify a vegetable's flavor by lightly sautéing before adding a broth

Temper: to bring a liquid (usually eggs) to a warmed state prior to mixing with another heated liquid

U-: as a measurement of weight, the number in a pound

Vinaigrette: light sauces of oil, vinegar, herbs, etc., to complement meats and vegetables

Water Bath: a vessel of hot water in which food-filled containers sit during cooking

Zest: the thin, colored rind portion of citrus fruits which contains the fruit's pungent oil

Conversion Chart

Liquid Measurements

Pinch : 1/16 to slightly less than ⅛ tablespoon
Dash : a few drops
Jigger : 3 tablespoons or 1 ½ ounces
1 teaspoon : ⅓ tablespoon
1 tablespoon : 3 teaspoons or ½ ounce
2 tablespoons : ⅛ cup or 1 ounce
4 tablespoons : ¼ cup or 2 ounces
5 tablespoons plus 1 teaspoon : ⅓ cup
8 tablespoons : ½ cup or 4 ounces
10 tablespoons plus 2 teaspoons : ⅔ cup
16 tablespoons : 1 cup or 8 ounces
⅛ cup : 1 ounce or 2 tablespoons
¼ cup : 2 ounces or 4 tablespoons
⅜ cup : ¼ cup plus 2 tablespoons
⅓ cup : 5 tablespoons plus 1 teaspoon
½ cup : 4 ounces or 8 tablespoons
⅝ cup : ½ cup plus 2 tablespoons
⅔ cup : 10 tablespoons plus 2 teaspoons
¾ cup : 6 ounces or 12 tablespoons
⅞ cup : ¾ cup plus 2 tablespoons
1 cup : 8 ounces or ½ pint
2 cups : 16 ounces or 1 pint
4 cups : 32 ounces or 2 pints or 1 quart
8 cups : 64 ounces or 4 pints or 2 quarts
1 pint : 2 cups or 16 ounces
1 quart : 4 cups or 2 pints or 32 ounces
1 gallon : 16 cups or 8 pints or 4 quarts

Estimating raw ingredients

To measure:		
Butter or fats	Follow charts above	
To measure:	*Dry Weight of 1 Cup*	*Weight = Volume*
Flour, all-purpose	4½ ounces	8 ounces = 1⅞ cups
Sugar, brown, packed	7 ounces	8 ounces = 1⅛ cups
Sugar, granulated	7 ounces	8 ounces = 1⅛ cups
Sugar, confectioners'	4½ ounces	8 ounces = 2 cups

INDEX